NICE TALK, GI.

A DICTIONARY OF MILITARY
TERMINOLOGY AND SLANG
FROM THE KOREAN WAR
TO THE VIETNAM ERA.

ROBERT V. HUNT, JR.

Order this book online at www.trafford.com
or email orders@trafford.com

Most Trafford titles are also available at major online book retailers.

Print information available on the last page.

ISBN: 978-1-6987-1472-1 (sc)
ISBN: 978-1-6987-1473-8 (e)

Trafford rev. 07/25/2023

 www.trafford.com

North America & international
toll-free: 844-688-6899 (USA & Canada)
fax: 812 355 4082

FOREWORD

This work doesn't claim to be an all-encompassing dictionary of terminology utilized by service personnel from Korea to Vietnam. No doubt that each unit that served in a war zone between 1950 and 1975 had its own vernacular, but many of the terms were common to all GIs during the wars in Korea and Southeast Asia. My apologies for not presenting the entire list of camps and stations occupied by the U.S. military during these eras, but there were too many to list, and the author has named those he was most familiar with and that were the most prominent.

Clarification: "Korea II" refers to U.S. and South Korean military actions against North Korean Communists, primarily between 1965 and 1971.

ALPHA

Alpha:	First letter of phonetic alphabet; the primary purpose of it was to make communication by radio/telephone more clear.
AACV:	Vietnam: Assault Air Cushion Vehicle. Both versions carried 12 combat-equipped soldiers. With all weather capacity, it possessed three times the fire power of a Huey Cobra gunship.
About Face:	180 degree pivot from a formation or individual standing at attention.
ACTIV:	Army Concept Team Vietnam: Designed to test new Army concepts under field conditions.
ACV:	Air Cushion Vehicle: Specifically built for U.S. Army to use in riverine warfare.
AC47 Dragonship:	USAF aircraft aka "Spooky" armed with miniguns.
AC119, 4C130:	Vietnam: USAF gunships with special electronic gear to detect enemy activities.
ACOFS:	Assistant Chief of Staff. Normally a lieutenant colonel commanding a staff section.
Acting Jack:	An enlisted man temporarily assuming a higher rank than actually achieved.
Active Duty:	Military personnel serving on a fulltime basis, often overseas in a warzone.

Adjust Fire:	Communicating to an artillery or mortar unit to change impact area of rounds.
Aerial Observer:	Korea I, Vietnam, Korea II: Light aircraft employed to spot for friendly forces.
Aerial Rifle Platoon:	Vietnam: Infantrymen assigned to 1st Air Cavalry units.
Aeromedical:	Personnel assigned to Military Airlift Command. Headquartered at Hickam AFV, Hawaii. 500,000th air evacuation of a patient occurred in February 1971.
After Action Reports:	Summary of events after a specific contact with the enemy. Often viewed as a learning tool for other units.
Affirmative:	Military term for "yes."
AFKN:	American (or Armed) Forces Korean Network. Transmitted radio and television programs for in-country personnel.
AFVN:	American (or Armed) Forces Vietnam Network. Ditto.
Agent Blue:	Vietnam, Korea II: Herbicide designed to destroy rice and other crops.
Agent Orange:	Dioxin: Herbicide chemical sprayed over 6 million acres in Vietnam and nearly 25,000 acres south of Korean DMZ. Purpose was to eliminate cover for enemy forces. Longstanding health problems associated with it.
Airborne:	U.S. Army soldiers trained to exit transport planes via static line attached to parachutes. Considered elite troops; many trained at Fort Benning, GA., and Fort Bragg, N.C.

Air Drop:	Resupplying ground troops with needed ammunition, food, water, etc.
Air Force:	U.S. military branch created in 1947; successor to Army Air Corps 1917-1947.
Air Medal:	Vietnam, Korea II: Awarded to helicopter crewmen after 25 combat hours, or after 50 regular flying hours or 50 supply hours.
Airmobile Operations:	Helicopter-borne tactical assaults. Began during Korean War and refined by U.S. Army in Vietnam.
Air Police:	USAF equivalent of military police.
AIT:	Advanced Individual Training. Also, Advanced Infantry Training.
All for one and one for all:	Vietnam: U.S. Army LRP motto.
Alert:	Warning to troops in garrison. Normally activated through a loudspeaker system.
All present and accounted for, sir:	Response by an NCO in charge of a platoon or unit when reporting to a superior officer about the status of his troops.
All the way, sir:	Snappy refrain showing elan or esprit de corps.
ALO:	Air Liaison Officer. Air force officers assigned to an Army unit.
Ambulance:	Military vehicle used to transport ill and wounded personnel. Normally olive drab in color with a red cross painted on the sides.
AN-PPS-4:	Radar used by GIs in Germany, Korea and Vietnam. Designed to detect enemy movement.

Anti-Tank Mines:	Designated M-7, M.15, and M-21.
AO:	Vietnam: Area of Operations.
AO Orange:	Vietnam: Area of operations of 1st Brigade, of 5th Mechanized Inf. Div. south of 17th parallel.
APC:	Armored Personnel Carrier (M-113). Vehicle developed for U.S. Army to carry a squad of soldiers. Used extensively during the Vietnam era. Lightly armored with one .50 caliber machine gun. Carried a crew of two, driver and gunner.
APC Formations:	(1) Column (2) Line (3) Wedge (4) Echelon.
APC Lights:	APCs and jeeps used black-tinted headlights in Vietnam and Korea II.
Appointment with the old man:	Enlisted man ordered to report to the commanding officer; not for social reasons.
ARA:	Air Rocket Artillery. Heavy ordnance designed to destroy helicopters and fixed wing aircraft.
ARCOM:	Army Commendation Medal. Awarded for exemplary meritorious or valorous performance.
ARADCOM:	Army Defense Command
Area Guard:	Individual detailed to guard a particular location or object.
Arizona:	Vietnam: USMC term for An Hon Valley southeast of Da Nang.
Arm and Hand Signals:	(1) Halt (hand straight up); (2) Enemy in sight (hold weapon in direction of enemy); (3) Assemble (rotate arm); (4) Cover my advance (tap top of head);

(5) Fire teams abreast (back stroke motion); (6) Attention (wave); (7) "Are you ready?"(Simulate pushing door); (8) Optional: Sighting of enemy (Using fingers to form letters "V" and "C."

Armed Chair Commando: Derogatory term for rear echelon soldiers.

Armed Forces Entrance
and Examination Station: Location of induction centers for processing new service members.

Armor Motto: "Plan deliberately; execute violently."

Armored Shorts: Vietnam: Briefs allegedly issued to Marines early in the war. Made of Teflon.

Armory Tents: Shelters used to store weapons, ammunition, etc.

Army: U.S. military branch created in 1775; charged with ground warfare and air warfare until 1947.

Army Air Mission
Commander: Vietnam: Officer in charge of helicopter strike force.

Army Five-in-
One Rations: Korean War-vintage food rations.

Army Issue: Basic equipment such as uniforms, supplies, weapons, etc. provided to fighting personnel.

Army Materiel
Command: Among other projects, it redesigned M-16 rifle in Oct. 1967. Originally designed for U.S. Air Force.

Army Reserve: Component of U.S. Army; not normally on active duty, but could be activated in wartime.

Article 15:	Non-judicial punishment imposed upon an enlisted man in lieu of a court-martial. Conviction often detailed a reduction in rank, extra duty, and forfeiture of pay.
Article 31:	Military equivalent of invoking 5th amendment protection.
Article 32:	Under UCMJ, premeditated murder.
Article 80:	Under UCMJ, Attempted murder.
Article 85:	Military personnel charged with desertion.
Article 88:	Individual serviceman charged with uttering contemptuous words against the president or other civilian officials.
Article 94:	Mutiny
Article 133:	Conduct unbecoming an officer
Article 134:	Under UCMJ, "Disloyal statements with intent to promote disaffection among the troops."
Artificial Sun:	ROK term for North Korean floodlights used to illuminate U.S. and friendly force positions along DMZ and manned islands off the coasts.
Artillery Ear:	Loss of hearing suffered by some Vietnam vets from long-term exposure to loud artillery explosions.
ARVN:	Army of the Republic of Vietnam, 1954-1975.
ASA:	Army Security Agency. Primary mission was to conduct surveillance and gather Intelligence.
Assistant CQ:	A charge of quarters detail at a unit's headquarters; normally performed by an enlisted man after regular duty hours.

Ass so tight:	Profanity usually followed by a bit of military hyperbole. As in "My ass was so tight you couldn't drive a jackhammer up."
ASAP:	As soon as possible. An acronym used frequently as in "The first sergeant wants to see you ASAP!"
ASCOM City:	Korea II: Acronym for "Army Support Command." A large U.S. Army base near Bupyang, South Korea. Also location of U.S. stockade, as well as the 121st Evacuation Hospital made famous in M*A*S*H television series 1972-1983.
Ass is Grass:	A little rhyme to indicate that someone is in big trouble.
Assault Ration:	Vietnam: Small cans of chow consumed by GIs in the field.
Ashau Valley:	Vietnam; Valley in northwestern South Vietnam near Laotian border. Site of much enemy activity.
As You Were:	Command to resume prior status or position.
ATC:	U.S. Army Training Center at Fort Sill, Oklahoma.
Attention or Atenhut!	Basic military directive for enlisted personnel to give undivided attention to the business at hand.

Authentication:	U.S. Army communication network: (1) Challenge & Reply (2) Self-Authentication (3) Message. Authentication Code Sheet: Used by officers and designated individuals in the field to provide secure communication of radio frequencies, passwords, etc.
Automatic Rifleman:	Korea, Vietnam, Korea II: Soldier or marine armed with an assault rifle, capable of firing multiple rounds at the pull of the trigger.
AWOL:	U.S. Army and U.S. Air Force; "Absent without leave." Service members away from assignment or duty station without permission.
AWOL Bag:	Small bag used by GIs to carry persona effects, often when on short term leave.
Azimuth:	"To shoot an azimuth." Employing a military compass to chart a direction from a baseline; used in the field to find an object or arrive at a destination.

BRAVO

Bravo:	Second letter of phonetic alphabet
Baby Bottles:	Vietnam: The real thing carried by USAF pilots as a survival aid.
Back Blast:	Explosion directed backward after a weapon is fired or detonated.
Bad of the Bad:	Vietnam: Sarin gas allegedly used in Laos in 1970 by U.S. Army personnel.
Bad Paper:	Term for a discharge from the military as a result of a court-martial conviction. Categories: Undesirable, Bad Conduct, and Dishonorable. GI with "bad paper" was normally denied VA benefits and faced civilian employment discrimination.
Bad Time:	Vietnam: GI term for extra duty as punishment for some perceived dereliction of duty.
Bald Ass Hill:	Korean War: Location of a pitched battle between North Korean and U.S. troops in 1.953.
Ba li-Ba li	Korean War: GI slang for "hurry, hurry."
Balls to the Walls:	Korean War: Term for employing extreme measures in a desperate situation.
Bamboo Mat:	Common sleeping surface in a NVA prison camp.

Banana Clip:	Rifle magazine holding 30 rounds; standard AK-47 assault rifle used by Communist forces. Later in Vietnam War 30-round magazine adopted for U.S. M-16, replacing 20-round magazine.
Bandoliers of Ammo:	Long, nylon fabric with pockets used to carry extra ammo magazines and often worn over or across the chest.
Banana Leaves:	Vietnam: Large tropical foliage often used as camouflage by enemy forces.
Bangalore Torpedoes:	Actually pre-Korea and Vietnam infantry weapon used against entrenched positions and personnel by Communist forces.
Banzai-GIs Die:	Korean War: North Korean assault troops screams to intimidate UNC personnel.
Barbed Wire Hotel (Resort):	GI lingo for stockade or brig.
Barracks:	World War II-era housing provided for GIs; normally a two-story white building with a latrine, showers and ten sets of top and bottom bunks on each floor. Very Spartan conditions.
(The) Barrier:	Korea II: Term for demilitarized zone (DMZ).
Base Exchange:	USAF version of PX or Post Exchange.
Base of Fire:	Infantry technique of saturating an area with heavy firepower to allow a unit to proceed or withdraw.
Basic School:	USMC: First steps in training a Marine.

Batcats:	Vietnam: USAF C-130s quipped with electronic eavesdropping capability on enemy communications.
Battalion:	U.S. Army, USMC units: Normally composed of three or more companies of 800 to 1,000 men.
Battle Dead:	U.S. military's official description of personnel killed in action against an enemy.
Battle Drill:	Training for combat situations.
Battle of the Bowling Alley:	Korean War: August 1950 battle between units of U. S. 2nd Inf. Div. and NKPA's 13th Inf. Div. Latter sustained some 4,000 casualties.
Battery:	Artillery unit, normally comprised of six or more howitzer pieces.
Battle Sight Zero:	Test firing a weapon – usually a rifle-to align sights so that bullets strike where aimed.
Bayonet:	Long-knife attached to end of a rifle. Used for close combat. Also nickname of U.S. Army's 7th Inf. Div.
Bayonet Country:	Korea II: Nickname for area controlled by U.S. Army's 7th Inf. Div.
BCD:	Bad Conduct Discharge.
BCT:	U.S. Army's Basic Combat Training. The introduction into military life required of every soldier.
BDA:	Vietnam: USAF, U.S. Navy, USMC: Bomb Damage Assessment.
Beat Feet:	Move out quickly, troop!

Beaucoup:	Vietnam: French term for many, much, more; part of GI lexicon. Antecedents traceable to Civil War; also used by American GIs in Europe in World War II and Korea I.
Bed Check Charlie:	Korean War: North Korean light plane flown near UNC positions in harass allied soldiers.
Beehive Rounds:	Vietnam: Lethal ordnance (sharp darts) fired by 155mm artillery to breakup human wave attacks.
Bell Telephone Hour:	Vietnam: Description of the use of electricity from a field telephone wire wrapped around vulnerable body parts of a suspected enemy to force him/her to divulge information. Hand-cranked power delivered a nasty shock.
Bend over grab your ankles and cough:	Jocular reference to BCT physical examination procedure.
Bent out of shape:	Semi-military term from the 1960s.
Betting his bars:	Term used by officers to indicate confidence that the right decision was made.
BFD:	Obscenity used by GIs as in "We're here again, we're here again, Big Fucking Deal"!
Bien Hoa:	Vietnam: Major city near Saigon that was site of many U.S. bases.
Big Chicken Dinner:	U.S. Navy term for Bad Conduct Discharge.
Big Ditch:	Korea II: Combat engineers name for Imjin River.
Billet:	Housing quarters, often temporary as when on R&R.

Bird-dog:	Vietnam, Korea II: Spotter Plane for friendly forces.
Birth Control Pills:	Vietnam, Korea II: GIs' factious term for malaria control pills.
Biscuit Bitches:	GI profanity for Red Cross girls.
Bites the Bag:	Semi-military term indicating that something is really bad.
Bivouac:	Training/camping in the field.
Black Barons:	Vietnam: Nickname for members of 269th Aviation Bn., 25th Inf. Div.
Black Belt:	Standard issue belt worn by U.S. soldiers during Vietnam era.
Black Box:	Vietnam: Sensor devices deployed to detect the movement of enemy personnel.
Black/Green Camouflage:	Korea, Vietnam, Korea II: Greasepaint worn by Special Forces, Rangers, Recon, etc. to disguise appearance in tactical situations.
Black Panther Highway:	Korea II: See Skyline Drive.
Black Horse:	Vietnam: Base 40 miles east of Saigon; home to 199th Light Infantry Brigade and 11th Armored Cav. Regt, 1965-1971.
Black Lions:	Vietnam: Regiment of 1st Inf. Div. First U.S. combat unit in WWI.
Black Market Alley:	District of Saigon, South Vietnam.
Black Pajamas:	Vietnam: Garb worn by many Viet Cong.
Black Virgin Mountain:	Vietnam: 3,200 feet elevation located in Tay Ninh Province. Site of major battles between U.S. and NVA troops.

Black Warfare:	Military tactics that likely violate conventional rules of warfare and civilized behavior.
Blanket Party:	Euphemistic description of a collective effort by trainees/recruits to punish a fellow soldier/recruit whose actions were deemed obnoxious or irritating enough to warrant overt punishment of some sort.
Blanks or Dummy Rounds:	Shells without gunpowder.
Blazing Skies Korea II:	Nickname for 38th artillery brigade.
Bleeding (types of):	(1) Capillary (2) Venous (3) Arterial.
Blocking Force:	Korea, Vietnam, Korea II: Infantry tactic to cut off an enemy retreat.
Bloody Ridge:	Korea: Site of ferocious fight between U.S. 2nd Inf. Div. and ROKA forces against NKPA. Friendly forces incurred 2,700 casualties.
Bloody Route 13:	Vietnam: Mine-infested road along Route 13 in Central Highlands.
Blousing Rubbers:	Hooked elastic bands, olive drab in color; used to keep trouser cuffs off fatigue or jungle trousers; secured above the top of combat/jungle boots.
BLT:	Battalion Landing Team (USMC).
Blues:	See Aerial Rifle Platoon.
Blue Line:	Topographical map symbol indicating water, stream or river.
Blue Suede shoes:	Korean War era: USMC term for combat boots.

Blue Team:	Vietnam: 1st Air Cav. units –many missions to help secure downed aircraft and crews.
Blue Water Navy:	Vietnam: U.S. naval vessels/personnel deployed in South China Sea and not in country.
Bobcats:	Vietnam: Nickname of 2nd Bn. of 5th Mechanized Inf. Div.
B-Med:	Battalion Medical Station.
Body Count:	Vietnam: Counting of enemy dead as a gauge of progress; idea that U.S. – and allied forces could kill more enemy than could be replaced. Originated with top civilian leaders in Johnson Administration.
Bodes:	Vietnam: GI term for Cambodians.
Bogy:	Korea, Vietnam: Aircrews name for an enemy fighter jet.
Bolo:	Failure to qualify on the rifle range.
Boom-Boom:	Sex with prostitutes.
Boom-Boom House:	GI term for Vietnamese house of prostitution.
Booby Trap:	A disguised or hidden device designed to inflict injury or death on enemy personnel.
Boon Dockers:	Korean War: USMC term for ankle boots.
Boonies:	Vietnam era: Activities in the field, i.e. the "boondocks."
Boonie or Bush Hats:	Floppy soft hats, olive drab or camouflage cover; worn by GIs in Vietnam and Korea II. Not officially sanctioned headgear.

Boonie Rats:	Grunts who spend most of their time in the field.
Boot Camp:	USMC version of BCT
Boots & Saddles:	Old First Cavalry bugle call.
BOQ:	Bachelor Officers Quarters.
Border Battles:	Vietnam: NVA term for offensives launched in 1968.
Bought the farm:	Vietnam: USAF term indicating someone killed in action.
Bouncing Betty:	German-designed. Later U.S. Army anti-personnel mine (M-16) used in Korea, Vietnam, Korea II. Designed to bounce waist-high before detonating.
Boxer Shorts:	Vietnam era: Underwear issued to trainees in Army Reception Center; jockey shorts not an acceptable alternative.
BRASS:	Acronym used in Army BCT and Marine boot camp to help trainees/recruits learn basic marksmanship with M-14 rifle. Stands for: Breath, Relax, Aim, Take up the slack and Squeeze the trigger.
Bravo Team:	U.S. Army, USMC; second group of soldiers in a ten-man squad.
Break Contact:	A unit moving away from enemy forces.
Breaking Squelch:	Vietnam: Using clicks on a tactical unit's PRC-25 radio to communicate with friendly forces in order to avoid giving away position to the enemy.
Break you down to build you up:	Premise of military training to turn a civilian into a combatant.

Bridge of No Return:	Korea II: Checkpoint #3 across Imjin River near Panmunjom.
Brigade:	Smallest self-sustaining Army/Marine unit that can be independently deployed. Approximately 3,000 men.
Bright Light Teams:	Vietnam: Special Forces personnel engaged in clandestine operations in Cambodia and Laos.
Bring smoke on your ass:	Generic threat by a superior to an inferior that he better shape up or he will pay a high price.
BROCAS:	U.S. Army: (1) Brief (2) Release to do job (3) Observe (4) Correct (5) Advise (6) Supervise.
Bronco Pilots:	Vietnam: U.S. Army pilots of small aircraft used primarily for surveillance.
Brown Boot Army:	Footgear worn by soldiers prior to 1956.
Brown Noser:	Term of disdain for those who curry favor with superiors.
Brown Water Navy:	Vietnam: U.S. Naval craft/personnel assigned to inland waterways of Mekong Delta.
Bubbling Bobbies:	H10 Chickasaw helicopter used by U.S. Army and USAF in period 1953-1971. Workhorse for rescue and supply operations in Korea. Used by USMC in Vietnam.
Bucking for a section eight:	Administrative discharge from the service – often for mental/personality problems.
Buck Private:	Soldier with no rank, aka Private E-1.
Buck Sergeant:	U.S. Army: NCO rank of E-5 (three hard stripes on shoulder sleeves).

Budda Grass:	Potent strain of marijuana smoked by GIs in Southeast Asia.
Buddy System:	Army practice of pairing soldiers to help each other to help maximize efficiency and morale.
Bug Out:	Vietnam: Infantryman's term for putting self-preservation and fear of certain death to prompt near-mutinous actions.
Bugging Out:	Korean War term for hasty retreat in face of imminent enemy threat.
Bu Kan:	North Koreans.
Bull's Eye:	Fired projectile striking dead center of a target.
Bunker Commander:	Vietnam, Korea II: Soldier assigned to direct activities in a fortified bunker.
Bunker Hill:	Vietnam: USMC battle in 1967; Marines sustained a large number of casualties.
Burmese Tiger Traps:	Sophisticated devices used by Communist forces in Southeast Asia; originally designed for animals, but also used against enemy personnel. Camouflaged holes with sharpened bamboo sticks pointing upward.
Burn Cage:	Special incinerator used to destroy classified paperwork after each work day to prevent enemy access.
Bush:	Vietnam, Korea II: Hostile fire areas.
Business Girls:	Vietnam, Korea II: Prostitutes.
Business Hours:	U.S. Navy, USMC term for enlisted personnel facing non-judicial punishment.

Busted:	Slang for official punishment, demotion
Busting Caps:	Vietnam, Korea II: Firing weapons at the enemy.
Butterfly:	Korea II: Term used by GIs to describe a prostitute or "Yo-bo" who cheated on GI "boyfriend" to earn extra cash.
Butterfly Bombs:	Vietnam: Anti-personnel explosives dropped on enemy troops.
Butt Can:	Vietnam era: Container in barracks used for disposing of cigarettes.
Butt Plate:	Rear compartment of a rifle; used for storing cleaning utensils, etc.
B-26s:	Korean War: Douglas Invader light bombers used for low-level bombing.
B-52s:	Vietnam: USAF stratofortress heavy bombers used for saturation bombing of enemy sites in Vietnam and along Cambodian and Laotian borders. Nickname Big Ugly Fellas.
B-57s:	Vietnam: USAF bombers deployed for secret bombing missions over Ho Chi Minh Trail.
Burst of Six:	Term of derision by non-career soldiers toward a career soldier re-enlisting for an additional six years of service.

CHARLIE

Charlie:	Third letter of phonetic alphabet.
CA:	Civil Affairs: U.S. Army unit assigned to deal with indigenous population.
CA:	Vietnam, Korea II: Combat Assault.
Cadence:	Verbal tool for teaching soldiers/recruits to march in unison: Ex: "I don't know but I've been told, old Fort Knox is filled with gold. Sound off, 1, 2, sound off 3, 4. Sound off, 1,2,3,4, 1-2, 3-4."
Cadre:	Term for instructors in BCT and AIT.
Cake walk:	Vietnam: Term supposedly said by a colonel in the 1st Air Cav. comparing Vietnam with his experiences in World War II and Korea.
Calamity Jane:	Vietnam: 155mm howitzers assigned to 11th artillery, 11th Army Regt. The "Golden Dragons" assigned to 101st Air Mobile Division.
Call Sign:	Communication designation. Ex: commanding officer always referred to as "6"and 1st sergeant as "7"via radio/telephone system.
Camaraderie:	Shared experiences or hardships leading to a unique bond among GIs.
Cammies:	Vietnam: Slang for camouflaged jungle fatigues.
Camouflage Cover:	Vietnam era: Cloth worn over steel pot helmets; woodland pattern on one side and desert pattern on the other.

Campaign Medal	Award given to service members serving honorably in a war zone.
Camp Alpha:	Vietnam: Largest R&R process center near Saigon.
Camp Carroll:	Korea II: Army Materials Command (AMC); largest repair depot in Far East. Equipment from Vietnam also sent for repair.
Camp JJ Carroll:	Vietnam: USMC base camp eight miles south of DMZ (17th parallel). Aka, "artillery plateau."
Camp Casey:	Korea II: Base camp of 7tn Inf. Div.
Camp Cochise: U.S. Artillery base in ROK.	U.S. Artillery base in ROK.
Camp Hovey:	Korea II: HQ 3rd Bde. 7th Inf. Div.
Camp Howze:	Korea II: HQ 2nd Inf. Div.
Camp Kaiser:	Korea II: HQ of 1st Bde. 7th Inf. Div.
Camp Lejeune:	USMC base located in North Carolina.
Camp Matta:	Korea II: 2nd Inf. Div. frontline camp.
Camp Pendleton:	USMC base located in California.
Camp Red Cloud:	Korea II: HQ of I Corps (Gp) near Uijongbu.
Camp Young:	Korea II: HQ 2nd Bde. 7th Inf. Div.
Camp Zama:	Japan: U.S. military hospital treating severely wounded GIs from Vietnam and Korea II.
Cam Ranh Bay:	Vietnam: Port and city on northeast coast of South Vietnam; considered one of safest areas during the war.
Can Do GI:	Pidgin English used by Koreans, Vietnamese civilians when dealing with GIs.

Cannon Cocker:	Nickname for personnel assigned to an artillery unit.
Cannoneers:	Members of a howitzer unit.
CAP:	Combat Air Patrol.
Captain:	A company grade officer in U.S. Army, USAF, and USMC. In U.S. Navy and Coast Guard the equivalent rank of colonel.
Captain's Mast:	U.S. Navy: Non-judicial punishment for enlisted personnel.
Carabiner:	Vietnam: Large metal claps used to secure equipment, or, more rarely, personnel.
Carrys:	U.S. Army: (1) Fireman (2) Pack Strap (3) Saddle Back (4) Pistol Belt.
Carry On:	Superior officer's order to a subordinate to resume normal activity
CAR-15:	Vietnam: Modified version of M-16 rifle often weapon of choice by LRRPs and Special Forces.
Catch a lot of flack:	Getting in trouble.
Cat Hole:	Small field latrine, roughly 12" deep.
Case of the Jaws:	Frustration or disgust with an order, directive or individual.
Cattle Trucks:	U.S. Army: Large semi-trucks used to transport trainees to training sites.
CBR:	Chemical, Biological, Radiological weapons.
CBU:	Vietnam: Cluster Bomb Unit.
CDG:	Vietnam: Civilian Irregular Defense Group. South Vietnamese forces created to protect villagers from Viet Cong.

CEV:	Combat Construction Vehicle. U.S. Army heavy tank-like vehicle with construction/destruction capabilities Equipped with 165mm gun.
Cedar Falls:	Vietnam: U.S. military campaign, 1967
Challenge and Reply:	Password system used to identify friendlies from enemy personnel; often used at night.
Chain of Command:	Order of authority in the military; premised on the idea that enlisted personnel should consult immediate superiors and not go over their heads with problems, complaints, etc.
Chain Gang:	Vietnam: Nickname of a platoon of 1st Bn. 502 Abn. Inf. 101st AMD.
Chang Yo:	Korean term for prostitute.
Chargers:	Vietnam: Members of 4th Bn. 31st Inf. 196th LIB.
Chapter 10 Discharges:	Mainly for enlisted personnel; 90% percent undesirable.
Charlie-Land:	Vietnam: Viet Cong areas.
Charlie-Charlie:	Phonetic alphabet designation for command and control.
Charm School:	An Khe, Vietnam: 1st Air Cav. training center
Check eyelids for holes:	Put-down of trainees/recruits who fell asleep sitting in bleachers during often boring lectures.
Check Fire:	Command (often urgent) for attacking force to cease fire because of events on the ground in order to avoid friendly casualties.

Chemical Nerve Agents:	(1) Nerve (2) Blister (3) Blood (4) Choking (5) Incapacity (6) Tear.
CH-46:	USMC Sea Knight; large cargo and troop moving helicopter used extensively in Vietnam.
CH-47:	U.S. Army twin-rotor heavy helicopter.
CH-53:	USMC Sea Stallion; larger version of CH-46.
CH-54:	U.S. Army heavy helicopter, aka Sky Crane.
Chinaman's Hat:	Korean War: Site of major battle between U.S. 2nd Inf. Div. and Chinese Communist forces in Nov. 1950.
Chicom:	Chinese Communists
Chicken Plate:	Vietnam, Korea II: Chest armor worn by helicopter pilots and crew members.
Chieu Ho:	Vietnam: "Open Arms" defector from Viet Cong.
Chiggy Bearers:	Korean war: Indigenous personnel hired to carry supplies to front-line troops.
Chogi Flights:	Korea II: Flights originating out of Osan AB to numerous Army and Air Force facilities in-country.
Chongo Street:	Korea: Notorious red-light district in Seoul.
Chop, chop, chop, chop:	GI escapees attempt to communicate with ARVN soldiers that they were Americans.
Chow Hall:	Structure where GIs ate meals when in garrison.
Chuck:	Vietnam: Black GIs term for whites.

CIB:	Korea, Vietnam, Korea II: Combat Infantryman's Badge. Coveted award earned by soldiers with extended time in combat; usually participating in at least five firefights.
CID:	U.S. Army and U.S. Air Force: Criminal Investigation Division. Authorized to seek out criminal activity committed by military personnel.
CIDG:	Vietnam: Civilian Irregular Defense Group.
CINCPAC:	U.S. Navy: Commander-in-Chief, Pacific.
CINCUSARPAC:	Commander-in-Chief U.S. Army Pacific. Vietnam era led by four-star general headquartered at Fort Shafter, Hawaii.
Cinderella Liberty:	USN/USMC: Liberty that ended at midnight
Circle Jerk:	Derogatory term implying certain GIs were not attending to business at hand. As in "Break up the circle jerk!"
City People:	Vietnam: Inhabitants of Saigon and other large cities who seemingly showed little appreciation of the sacrifices of the South Vietnamese military.
Civic Action:	Vietnam, Korea II: Pacification efforts to "win hearts and minds" of indigenous population.
Civies:	GI term for non-military clothes.
Clacking bamboo sticks together:	Vietnam: Viet Cong means of communication.

Class A Uniforms:	Dress green uniforms worn by soldiers on formal occasions and sometimes during travel between assignments. Other service members wore own version.
Claymore:	U.S. Army-designed anti-personnel mine. Rectangular 8" x 10" size containing 800 ball bearings detonated by C-4 plastic explosive.
Clean Speech Month:	Vietnam: Base camp commander's campaign to encourage GIs to avoid profanity as much as possible. Of dubious value.
Clear and Hold:	Vietnam: Tactic of eliminating VC influence in a village and assigning South Vietnamese forces to maintain security against VC.
Clear Weapon:	Making certain that a round was not chambered and accidentally discharged.
Clover Leaf Recon:	Vietnam: Searching for enemy positions by personnel using a systematic, overlapping tactic.
Cluster Fuck:	Vulgarity urging GIs to spread out so as not to make themselves vulnerable in case of contact.
Coke Cans:	U.S. Army: Accessory used in some training bases to insure that towels were rolled properly.
C-O-L-D:	Acronym used to help soldiers avoid hypothermia, frostbite and trench foot. (1) Cleanliness (2) Overheating (3) Layers (4) Dampness
College Boys:	Vietnam: CIA personnel.

Column Left, Column Right:	Directions ordered to trainees/recruits to follow when marching in formation.
COM:	Vietnam: Concerned Officer Movement. A loosely organized antiwar movement of Army and USMC officers.
Combat Action Ribbon:	USMC equivalent of CIB.
Combat Boots:	Standard issue military footgear
Combat Clerks:	Vietnam, Korea II: Men assigned to a non-combat MOS who could possibly find themselves in a combat situation.
Combat Fox:	Korea II (1968): USAF airlift during *USS Pueblo* crisis. Largest airlift in USAF history. Surpassed airlift of 101st ABD to Vietnam in 1967.
Combat Load:	Assigned amount of gear and ammunition to be carried in the field. In Vietnam, soldiers sometimes carried 60-80 pound loads.
Combined Action Platoon:	Vietnam: USMC units.
Commander:	In the chain of command, the officer in charge of a unit.
Command Decision:	Action of a senior commander to make an important decision.
Command Inspection:	A major evaluation of personnel, equipment, facilities, etc. by senior officers.
Command Voice:	Distinctive tone and delivery intended to elicit respect and obedience.
Commander of Relief:	Officer in charge of substituting for regular officers during off-duty hours

Commo Lines:	Common User Telephone: Communication equipment and transmission between units.
COMNAFOR Korea:	Korea II: Commander, Naval Forces, Korea.
Company:	Basic military unit. In Army and USMC normally comprised of three or four platoons.
Company Grade:	U.S. Army, USMC, USAF: 2nd lieutenants, 1st lieutenants and captains. Thus the lowest ranking officers.
Company Street:	Narrow lanes between buildings on a military installation.
Compass Equipment:	Korea, Vietnam, Korea II: Instruments used in land navigation – possibly acetate map, grease, pencil, protractor, and compass.
Compound:	Barracks, offices, mess halls, etc. of a military facility.
Conduct unbecoming an officer:	Gross dereliction of duty on the part of a commissioned officer.
CO:	Commanding Officer: at the company level normally a captain.
Cone of Fire:	Projection of lethality; usually associated with weapons that fire at a constant or automatic rate.
Con Son:	Vietnam: See Tiger Cages
Contact:	Encountering enemy personnel or armaments.
Con Thien:	Vietnam: USMC base 2 ½ miles south of DMZ.

Coney Island:	Vietnam: Soldiers derogatory term for Marines alleged propensity to use too much illumination at the Khe Sanh siege in 1968.
CONEX:	Large steel containers used to transport materials.
Containing Communism:	Credo of U.S. forces Korea I to Vietnam to Korea II.
Conventional Armaments:	Standard munitions as opposed to nuclear, biological or chemical weapons.
CONUS:	Continental United States.
Cook(s):	Vital component of military life; difficult to sustain any activity without adequately-fed service members.
Cook Off:	A defective round exploding inside the barrel of a weapon.
Copping Zees:	Sleeping when on Guard duty, listening post, observation post, etc.
Corpsman:	Vietnam: Naval personnel who performed First aid for Marines in the field.
COSVN:	Vietnam: Central Office for South Vietnam; considered headquarters of National Liberation Front (NLF) in 1970. Located in Cambodia near border with South Vietnam.
Cotton Balls:	Vietnam: NVA AAA tracers fired at allied aircraft.
Cover and Concealment:	Combat troops using natural terrain and foliage for protection against enemy fire.
CQ:	Charge of Quarters.

C- Rats:	GI term for C-Rations, aka canned or combat rations.
Criminal Acts:	Korea II: NKPA term for alleged U.S. misdeeds. Vitriol exchanged at Panmunjom.
Crew Served Weapons:	Heavy weapons requiring multiple personnel to function effectively.
Crusaders:	Vietnam: Gung-ho GI who believed in U.S. mission to contain communism and protect South Vietnam.
CSDB:	Combined Services Disciplinary Barracks, Leavenworth, Kansas.
CTT:	Combat Tracker Teams: Vietnam, Korea II: Dog units introduced into Vietnam in 1967 and Korea in 1968, working with infantry units.
Curfew:	Vietnam, Korea II: Time when civilians and unauthorized military personnel had to be off the streets for security reasons. In major cities of Vietnam, curfew hours varied, depending on level of threat. In Korea, it was 1200 to 0400 hours in areas north of Seoul. Expanded during times of overt North Korean aggression.
Currency Violations:	Vietnam, Korea II: Failure to exchange Federal Reserve Notes for MPC (military payment currency) could result in a maximum penalty of three years in prison and a dishonorable discharge. Idea of exchange being to combat black market activities in host country.

Cut me some slack:	Slang for "Take it easy, chief, I'm only human."
Cunt Cap:	Vulgar name for U.S. Army, USMC, USAF garrison cap.
Cut a Chogie:	Korea, Korea II: GI slang for moving out quickly, or retreating in face of enemy threat.
Cut Orders:	Official assignment to next duty station.
CWS:	Korea II: Counter-Guerrilla Warfare school located at 7th Inf. Div. headquarters.
CYA:	"Cover Your Ass." Action to avoid blame if anything goes wrong.
C-119, C-130:	USAF gunships with special electronic gear.
C-130:	USAF Loadmaster. Multipurpose cargo aircraft.
C-141:	USAF transport planes flown during Vietnam era.
Cyclo:	Vietnam: Tricycles used to transport passengers.

DELTA

Delta:	Fourth letter of phonetic alphabet
Daisy Chain:	Vietnam, Korea II: Claymore mines connected by det cord to ignite a simultaneous explosion.
Daisy Cutter:	Vietnam: USAF: 15,000-lb bomb used to clear the jungle for landing zones.
Dak to:	Vietnam: City in Central Highlands; site of many battles at the height of the war.
Daniel Boone:	Vietnam: Special Forces units sent on covert operations into Cambodia.
Daylight Reconnaissance Patrol:	Vietnam, Korea II: Small unit sent out to determine enemy tactical situation.
Da Nang:	Vietnam: Large city on coast some 150 miles northeast of Saigon; site of major USMC and USAF and Army bases.
DASC:	Korea II: Direct Air Support Center at Osan, AB. Coordinated close air support for ground troops.
Day Room:	Area in barracks set aside for off-duty GIs to relax.
Davy Crockett:	U.S. Army-designed bazooka tested in early to mid-1950s. Each round tipped with 7 ounces of depleted uranium. Residual rounds still exist at Army bases in CONUS and Hawaii.
DD:	Dishonorable Discharge.
DD214:	U.S. military members permanent service record.

Death Bees:	GI lingo for bullets.
DECOMPSAMAC:	Vietnam: Deputy Commander, U.S. Military Command.
Defensive Targets:	Vietnam, Korea II: Friendly artillery fire designed to discourage enemy probe attacks.
Demolition Pay:	Vietnam, Korea II: Extra pay for EOD personnel. Officers received $110 a month and EMs $55.
Demoralizer:	U.S. Army's Eight-inch self-propelled howitzer.
Department of the Navy:	U.S. military branch created in 1775.
DEROS:	Date Eligible to Return from Overseas Service.
DEROS Calendar:	See short-timer calendar.
Detachment B-57:	Vietnam: U.S. Army intelligence gathering and counter-intelligence operations; members assigned to Military Intelligence Corps.
Detail:	Assignment given to enlisted personnel; often involving menial tasks.
Detect Enemy Camouflage:	Searching for (1) Blend (2) Shape (3) Size (4) Texture (5) Color (6) Movement (7) Shine (8) Tone
Devil's Alley:	Seoul, South Korea: Area notorious for black market activities.
Devil's in Baggy Pants:	Nickname of 2nd Bn. 504th Inf. 82nd ABD.
Devil Dogs:	Nickname for Marines.
Deuce and a Half:	U.S. Army: GI term for two and one-half ton all-purpose truck.

Dex Tabs:	Vietnam: Dexedrine tablets used by some field troops to stay awake at night.
Didi:	Vietnamese term for "move out" or "hurry."
Diddly Squat:	Throw away term: As in "I don't give a diddly squat."
Diesel Cans:	A detail performed by GIs to keep diesel-fueled stoves functioning in hooches, barracks, tents, etc.
Diseases GIs exposed to in Asia war zones:	Cholera, Dengue Fever, Diphtheria, Dysentery, Encephalitis, Gonorrhea, Hemorrhagic Fever, Influenza, Jungle Rot, Leprosy, Malaria, Meningitis, Plague, Rabies, Skin diseases, Syphilis, Tetanus, Trench foot, Tuberculosis, Typhoid, Yellow Fever, Yellow Jaundice.
Miscellaneous Threats:	Agent Blue, Agent Orange, Agent White, Anthrax, asbestos, CBR, Coal Briquets, DDT, Depleted Uranium, Diesel Fumes, Nerve Agents, Smog, Snakes, Leeches, Tactical Nuclear Weapons, Animals.
Dismissed:	Officer separated from the military for dereliction of duty. Also, an officer ending a formal conversation with subordinate personnel. Ex: "Specialist Jones, you are dismissed."
Dismounted Drill:	Training purpose: (1) Teamwork (2) Discipline (3) Confidence (4) Esprit de Corps (5) Solid performance to increase combat qualification.

Dishonorable Discharge:	Military equivalent of a felony conviction.
Dispensary:	Company-level medical unit.
DivArty:	Division Artillery.
DMZ:	Vietnam: "Dead Marine zone."
DMZ:	Demilitarized zone; In Korea it roughly followed 38th parallel; in Vietnam, roughly followed 17th parallel. Misnomer: These areas were actually highly militarized. Korean DMZ contained some one million mines, antipersonnel and anti-tank, on both sides.
Doggies:	Korea: Marine's semi-contemptuous term for soldiers.
Dog Patch:	Vietnam: Villages outside U.S. bases; often created to cater to physical needs of GIs.
Dog Tags:	Small metal identification plates worn by a GI on his person. Often on a chain around the neck, but also on helmet, pack, boots, etc. Tag included name, service number, blood type and religion.
Dong Ha:	Vietnam: USMC base near DMZ.
Donkey Dicks:	Korea: GI slang for hot dogs.
Donut Dollies:	Vietnam, Korea II: GI term for Red Cross girls who dispensed treats and entertainment at combat bases.
Dose of the Green Wienie:	GI sarcastic term for U.S. Army.
Double Digit Midget:	Service members counting down to DEROS date. Thus fewer than 100 days left in his tour.

Do the Dap:	Distinctive handshake practiced by many black GIs.
Double Time:	Moving out quickly, i.e. running.
Draft Dodger:	Vietnam era: Young men who used all means-legal and otherwise-to avoid military service.
Dragon Head:	Korea II: Area of Imjin river south of DMZ; site of many firefights.
Dragon Missile:	Shoulder-fired weapon capable of destroying armor and field fortifications.
Dress Right Dress:	Technique for organizing a platoon of soldiers in a formation. Four rows: 1st row (one squad) takes two steps forward; 2nd row (one squad) takes one step forward; 3rd row (one squad) stands still; 4th row (one squad) takes one step backward. Soldiers then extend right arm so outstretched fingers barely touch shoulder of man to the right. Platoon then called to attention.
Drill Instructor:	USMC: NCOs assigned to guide recruits through boot camp.
Drill Sergeant:	Army NCOs assigned to guide trainees through BCT and AIT.
Drop on Down:	Order for a trainee/recruit to assume the front leaning rest position to begin a series of pushups.
Dress Code:	Standards for apparel worn by service members on and off-duty.
Ducks:	Korea: Amphibious vehicles used to land troops and supplies.

Duffle Bag:	Large, olive drab bag with handles and secured by a padlock to carry a GI's personal gear, uniforms, etc.
Dumbo:	Vietnam: SA-16 twin-engine amphibious plane.
Dungarees:	USMC work uniform.
Dust off:	Korea, Vietnam, Korea II: Helicopter borne emergency evacuation of wounded or ill soldiers/marines.
Dusters:	Vietnam: M42A chassis mounted with twin 40mm cannons. Sometimes used as anti-personnel weapons.
DTOC:	U.S. Army: Division Tactical Operations Center.
Duty Roster:	Post daily at company level detailing extra work to be performed by designated personnel.
Duty Officer:	Officer assigned to handle all eventualities on a military base between 1600 hours and 0800 hours.
Duty Station:	Assignment, usually for a specified time; often at least 12 months.
DX:	Direct exchange of units in the field.
DZ:	Korea, Vietnam, Korea II: Drop Zone.
D7E or D8:	U.S. Army caterpillar tractors.
Dye Marker:	Vietnam: Army & Marine operations in I Corps; also, Army Chemical Co. based at Camp Red Cloud, Korea.

ECHO

Echo:	Fifth letter of phonetic alphabet.
Early Out:	Vietnam, Korea II: Option given to GIs serving a short tour in a war zone. Option to extend tour and receive an early discharge.
Eat the Apple and Fuck the Corps:	Marine derogatory term for USMC.
Edewa:	Korean for "Come here!"
Eighth Army:	Korea, Korea II: Main bastion of Army deployment- Gen. Matthew Ridgway called it the "Magnificent Eighth Army."
Eighth Infantry Division:	U.S. Army unit assigned to Germany during Vietnam era. Nicknamed "Pathfinders."
Eighty-eight Percent:	Vietnam: Percentage of GIs serving in 1968 who held a non-combat MOS.
Eightieth TFW:	Korea II: USAF unit at Kunsan, AB
Elbows and Asses:	What training NCOS wanted to see when trainees/recruits were policing the company area for cigarette butts, litter, etc.
Elevation:	On topographical maps the symbol for height. Or, adjusting a weapon's round impact area vertically.
Eleven Bravo:	U.S. Amy combat MOS (11B10) Light Weapons Infantryman.
Eleven 840 Rockets:	Vietnam: Anti-personnel and antivehicle weapon employed by enemy forces.

Eleventh Armored Cavalry Regiment:	Vietnam: U.S. Army unit nicknamed "Black Horse." HQ at Xuan Loc, 1967-1971.
Eleventh Infantry Brigade:	Vietnam: Unit attached to American Division. Nicknamed "Jungle Warriors." In-country 1967-1971.
EM:	Enlisted Men.
Enfilade Fire:	Axis of a target corresponds to axis of beaten zone of fire.
Equipment:	U.S. Army's classification of scout and sentry dogs-thus disposable.
Erroneous Scuttlebutt:	Rumor and misinformation filtered through the ranks. Ex: 7th Inf. Div. lost its colors during Korean War when overrun by Chinese Communists. Actually, it was the 1st Cav.7th Cav. Regt.
Entrenching Tool:	Small shovel carried by soldiers/marines to dig foxholes, latrines, etc.
EOD(Teams):	Korea, Vietnam, Korea II: Explosive Ordnance Disposal. Hazardous duty that involved finding, disarming and disposing of lethal explosives.
Escape and Evasion:	Vietnam era: Training taught to military personnel to avoid capture in a war zone.
ETS:	Expiration Term of Service.
Everybody Up:	Common command in BCT and AIT to compel trainees/recruits to get out of the sack and begin another day of training.

Expendable:	Vietnam: Fate of some GIs involved in siege of Ben Het in 1969. Accusation by father of an officer that his son and his men were abandoned by the Army.
Expendables:	Vietnam: Chopper pilots' Jargon for those who could –unofficially – be sacrificed if need be.
Expert:	Highest marksmanship category.
Exercise Focus Retina:	Korea II: March 1969: 800 paratroopers of 82nd ABD embarked at Fort Bragg, N.C. and flew non-stop on C-130 Hercules aircraft and jumped south of Han River, South Korea.
Execute Violently:	Deadly force to achieve an objective.
Expected:	Vietnam: Nurse triage term for wounded GIs expected to die.
Expedient Method:	EOD teams' technique to destroy mines and explosives-often using dynamite.
Extraction:	Vietnam, Korea II: Using a helicopter to pull personnel out of a dangerous combat situation.
Eyeball:	First person contact with the enemy.
Eyeglass Suspenders:	Black elastic band issued to GIs to keep glasses secured to the head.

FOXTROT

Foxtrot:	Sixth letter of phonetic alphabet.
FA Field Artillery:	During Korean War UNC forces fired some 7,693,909 rounds April-July 1953.
FAC:	Forward Air Controller.
Fart Sacks:	Korea: USMC term for sleeping bags.
Fall Back:	Controlled, disciplined retreat.
Fall in, Fall out:	Command for soldiers to assemble for a formation or disperse from a formation.
Fast Movers:	Vietnam, Korea II: (USAF) GI jargon for fighter jets, particularly F-4 Phantom fighter-bombers used for close air support.
Fat-fingered:	U.S. Navy: Navigation error caused by entering incorrect coordinates.
FDC:	Fire Detection Center. Support element controlling direction of artillery fire, close air support, etc.
FEBA:	Forward Edge of Battle.
FGU:	Vietnam: Friendly Guerrilla Unit.
Field Grade:	Military officers from the rank of major to colonel.
Field Grade Article 15:	Vietnam: Punishment imposed on an officer above the grade of captain.
Field Grade Article 18:	Severe punishment of officers.
Field Jacket:	M-65 olive drab military jacket issued to all enlisted personnel. Worn in colder weather and often used with a liner.
Field Mess:	Chow bought to soldiers in the field.

Field Stripped:	Breaking down a weapon or other military equipment to its basic parts for inspection, cleaning or repair. Also to dispose of items such as cigarettes to avoid giving a position away.
Fields of Fire:	Fire concentrated to achieve maximum effectiveness against an enemy target.
Fighting Fifth:	Nickname for USAF 5th Air Force. The most decorated Air Force unit. Gained fame in WW II and Korea. All time jet ace, Joe McConnell, shot down 16 MiGs and damaged five others during Korean War.
Fifth Mechanized Infantry Division:	Vietnam: U.S. Army unit nicknamed "Red Devils." Assigned to Quang Tri Combat Base 1969-1971.
Fill Week:	First week of Army BCT, where trainees were tested, inoculated, issued uniforms, etc.
Finger Method:	Technique for estimating distance on a topographical map.
Firebase:	Vietnam: Tactical outpost manned by U.S. and friendly forces, often in remote, enemy-infested areas.
Firebirds:	Vietnam: Nickname of 196th LIB's Aviation Co.
Fire Brigade:	Vietnam: Elite forces such as the 173rd Airborne Brigade and 101st ABD.
Firefly:	Vietnam: LOH Scout helicopter equipped with a searchlight.
Fire for effect:	Discharging weapons to elicit a response from the enemy.

Fire Guard:	U.S. Army: Security pulled in barracks during training. Normally one soldier awake on each floor of a two-story barracks at night, each serving one hour shifts. Idea to have someone on alert in case of fire. Also taught sleep deprivation.
Fireman's Carry:	Technique for pulling a wounded soldier over one's shoulder to move him to safety.
Fire Mission:	Concentrated expenditure of ordnance against enemy personnel, positions.
Fire and Maneuver:	Infantry tactic of firing, moving, seeking cover and repeating the process until an enemy force is neutralized.
Fire and Movement:	Similar tactic by a different name.
Fire Team:	U.S. Army and USMC: Half of a squad of infantry deployed in a combat formation; normally five men led by an E-4.
Fire Registration Process:	Vietnam: Military personnel assigned to track incoming and outgoing fire.
Fire Watch:	USMC equivalent of fireguard.
First Cavalry Division:	U.S. Army unit serving in Korea from 1950 to 1965. In Korean War sustained 3,811 KIAs.
First Air Cavalry Division:	Vietnam: "The First Team." U.S. Army airmobile division in-country 1965-1971. Sustained 5,521 casualties. Allegedly responsible for half of enemy KIA.
First Aviation Brigade:	Vietnam: Nickname the "Golden Hawks."

First Division Bunkers;	Vietnam: Bunker design taught to trainees in AIT. Designed by Gen. Dupuy of 1st Inf. Div. Featured a berm with interlocking firing holes.
First Face:	First Sergeant.
First Infantry Division:'	Vietnam: Nickname "The Big Red One." Motto: "Duty First." In-country 1965-1970.
First Lady of Vietnam:	Entertainer Martha Ray, who made numerous trips to visit the troops.
First Marine Division:	Served in Korea and Vietnam. The "Old Breed" served in the latter 1965-1971.
First Pig, First Shirt, First Sleeve	Slang for First Sergeant.
First Sergeant:	Senior NCO at the company level, normally an E-8.
Fire in the Hole:	Warning that a grenade or other explosive device was about to be detonated nearby.
Fishhook:	Vietnam: Area 50 miles northwest of Saigon; site of COSVN headquarters.
FIST:	Vietnam: Fire Support Team.
Five by Five:	Military truck
Five S's:	Procedure for securing POWs: (1) Search (2) Silence (3) Segregate (4) Speed (5) Safeguard.
Five-Star Pattern:	Vietnam, Korea II: 105mm howitzer tactical set up.
Flak Jacket:	Vietnam, Korea II: Protective vest designed to shield combatants from shrapnel.

Flaming Dart l:	Vietnam: U.S. reprisal attacks against North Vietnam, Oct-Nov 1965.
Flank Security:	Korea, Vietnam: Infantry unit providing tactical security for a larger unit.
Flare Ship:	Vietnam: Helicopters designed to saturate an area with flares.
Flash Suppressor:	Mechanical device secured to front of a rifle to minimize light from a muzzle blast. Idea to prevent enemy from honing in on the source.
Fleshette rockets:	Vietnam: Razor-sharp anti-personnel darts fired by U.S. aircraft.
Flight Status:	Personnel authorized to operate a helicopter or aircraft.
F LP:	Korea II: Front Line Ambulance.
Flying A-Frames:	Korea; GI term for resupply planes.
Flying Ass and Trash:	Vietnam, Korea II: Routine helicopter duties.
Flying Boxcars:	U.S. Air Force C-131s
Flying Telephone Poles:	Vietnam: USAF, U S N, USMC pilots' term for North Vietnamese SAMs (surface to air missiles).
FO:	Vietnam: Forward Observer. Assigned to observe enemy positions for arty units.
Follow Me:	Motto of U.S. Army infantry.
Foo Gas:	Vietnam: Aviation fuel combined with Naphtha (chemical) similar to napalm. Often stored in 55 gallon drums placed outside firebases to discourage enemy attacks.
Footgear:	Boots, shoes, overshoes that are standard issue to GIs.

Footlocker:	Wooden container, secured by a padlock, designed to hold a GI's personal property and clothing items. Placed at foot of a bunk or cot.
Footlocker P.T.:	Airborne training. A harassment that compelled would-be paratroopers to lift full footlockers overhead for long periods of time.
Forced March:	Compelling a military unit to walk as fast as possible at route step pace in order to reach an objective.
Forest Penetrator:	Vietnam: Weighted device designed to penetrate thick jungle to rescue men on the ground, often by helicopter.
Formation:	Soldiers organized for duty as in "Don't be late for formation."
Fourth Man Back:	Vietnam, Korea II: Many carrying an M-60 machine gun; often placed near middle of squad behind the point man and his slack.
Fort Benjamin Harrison:	U.S. Army base in Indiana where advanced military journalism was taught.
Fort Benning:	U.S. Army base in Georgia; home of infantry and airborne training.
Fort Bliss:	U.S. Army base in Texas and New Mexico.
Fort Bragg:	U.S. Army base in North Carolina. Home of 82nd ABD and JFK Special Forces Center.
Fort Campbell:	U.S. Army base in Kentucky and Tennessee. Home of 101st ABD.
Fort Carson:	U.S. Army base in Colorado.
Fort Dix:	U.S. Army base in New Jersey.

Fort Dix 38:	GIs involved in a riot at the stockade in June 1969.
Fort Gordon:	U.S. Army base in Georgia.
Fort Knox:	U.S. Army base in Kentucky; main armor training center.
Fort Lewis:	U.S. Army base in Washington; main departure-arrival location for soldiers assigned to Asian theaters during Vietnam era from 1968 on.
Fort Leonard Wood:	U.S. Army base in Missouri.
Fort Ord:	U.S. Army base in California.
Fort Polk:	U.S. Army base in Louisiana. A main training base for infantry soldiers assigned to Asian war zones.
Fort Riley:	U.S. Army base in Kansas.
Fort Stewart:	U.S. Army base in Georgia.
Foul Balls:	U.S. Army soldiers unable or unwilling to follow rules and regulations. Often on the road to dishonorable discharge.
Four Life Saving Steps:	(1) Clear air passages (2) Stop the bleeding (3) Treat or prevent shock (4) Protect the wound.
Fourth Infantry Division:	Vietnam: U.S. Army unit; nicknamed "Ivy Division." In-country 1966-1970.
Foxhole:	Small depression dug by GIs for protection from enemy fire.
FNG:	Vietnam: "Fucking New Guy."
FPL:	Korea, Vietnam, Korea II: Final Protective Line. The demarcation between friendly and enemy territory.
FP, L-R P, I:	Vietnam: Food Packet, Long-Range Patrol, Individual. Pre-cooked and dehydrated rations. aka LRRP rations.

Fragging:	From fragmentation grenades. Term made notorious in Vietnam era. Killing or wounding an NCO or officer in order to punish/intimidate for perceived harassment or unnecessarily dangerous assignments. Also used to harass or kill other soldiers and civilians. Particularly prevalent 1969-1971.
Freedom Bird:	Vietnam, Korea II: Civilian airliner transporting GIs from a war zone.
Freedom Hill:	Vietnam: USMC Replacement Depot in Da Nang.
Free Fire Zone:	Vietnam: Areas considered to be enemy territory and thus anyone found in the area subject to attack.
Freedom's Frontier:	Vietnam, Korea II: Term to reflect the belief that U.S. forces were containing Communism in Asia.
Freedom Vault:	Korea II: Feb 1971. 82nd ABD exercise transporting 700 paratroopers 8,500 miles from Fort Bragg, N.C. to drop area near Osan, South Korea.
Free World Forces:	U.S. and allies in Southeast Asia and the Far East.
Friction Tape:	Tape used to secure a weapon or equipment, often to minimize noise.
Friendlies:	GI term for fellow GIs. Used in combat situations by soldiers returning to a firebase or camp to identify themselves and not be mistaken for the enemy.
Fruit Salad:	Slang for abundance of service ribbons worn on Class A uniforms.

FTA:	Vulgarity made notorious during Vietnam: "Fuck the Army."
Fucking A:	Vulgarity meaning, "You better believe it."
Fuck you GI dog:	Vulgarity sometimes hurled at GIs by hostile prostitutes angered over some perceived slight or refusal to patronize their services.
Fucking Ten, went to shit and the dogs ate them:	Korea II: GI expletives.
Fuck up your health record:	USMC jargon for getting killed or seriously wounded.
Full Bird:	Officer in U.S. Army, Air Force and USMC with rank of colonel.
Full Metal Jacket:	USMC term for 7.62mm NATO rounds used in M-14 and M-60 weapons.
Free the Army:	Vietnam era. Anti-war exercise by activists at Fort Lewis, WA. in 1971. Members rowed across American Lake and were promptly arrested.
Friend Seekers:	Vietnam: Women who wanted to meet wealthy foreigners.
Front Leaning Rest:	Beginning position for a pushup.
Front Towards Enemy:	Embossed words on front of a Claymore mine to insure it detonated in correct direction.
FSB:	Vietnam: Fire Support Base.
Fuel Blivit Berms:	Vietnam: Carved out areas to secure fuel supplies to protect them from enemy fire.

Funky Fourth:	Vietnam: Derogatory term for 4th Inf. Div.
Funny Faces:	M-17 gas masks.
Funny Money:	Military Payment Certificates. Issued in lieu of greenbacks to fight black market corruption.
FTX:	Korea II: Field Training Exercise.
477th Army Hospital:	Korea II: Only veterinarian hospital in Korea.

GOLF

Golf:	Seventh letter of phonetic alphabet.
Gainesburgers:	Vietnam: GI term for chow.
GB Nerve Gas aka Tabun:	German-created in WW II: Stored by U.S. forces in forward areas during Cold War.
Geckos:	Vietnam: "Fuck you lizard," from the sound they made in the bush, especially at night.
Gem (The):	Eighth Army Depot Command, located near Taegu, South Korea, aka Camp Carroll.
Geneva Conventions Card:	Identification card carried by armed forces members in event of capture to hopefully provide for humane treatment.
General Orders:	Orders that apply to all military personnel on a regular basis.
Get out the peter meter and check the angle of the dangle:	Fairly jocular GI humor
Get somebody by the short-hairs:	Phrase indicating putting pressure on someone to the point of pain.
General Court-Martial:	Highest military tribunal; empowered to hand down the death sentence to GIs.
Geographic Orientation:	"Knowing where you are on the ground.
Geronimo I:	Vietnam: Military operation near Tuy Hoa Oct-Dec. 1966.

GHOSTING

Ghosting:	Vietnam, Korea II: GI s hiding out in rear areas to avoid duty.
Ghost Tunnel (Texas Street):	Korea II: Street in Seoul; also PX alley in Pusan, and Yankee Market in Taegu. All were black market meccas.
GI:	Nickname for military personnel. GI, likely Government Issue
GI Barracks:	Top to bottom cleaning of a barracks or other structure.
Gigs:	Demerits for infractions committed in training. Ex: Failure to shine boots, make bunk properly, keep brass polished, shirt pockets buttoned, etc.
GI Joe:	Term first appeared in Army newspaper *Yank* in June 1942.
Go Devils:	Vietnam: Nickname for 6th Bn. 31st Inf. 3th Bde. 9th Inf. Div.
Go Downtown:	Vietnam: USAF term for bombing targets in and around Hanoi, North Vietnam. Attacks were off-limits during Operation Rolling Thunder, 1965-1968.
Go Groundhog:	Vietnam: LRRPs, Rangers, Special Forces. Hiding from enemy until safe to continue mission.
Go into the Army/ Navy/Marines/Air Force or go to jail:	Option given to certain draft-age miscreants at height of Vietnam War.
Golf Course:	Vietnam: An Khe, home of 1st Air Cav.
Gooks:	Derived from Korean name for themselves, i.e. *Han-guk*. Evolved into a derogatory term for Asians.

Gook-Goosers:	Rockets fired by Marine aircraft.
Goodyear Lips:	Korea II: Vulgarity for black GIs.
Go Winchester:	USAF slang for fighter jet or other armed aircraft running out of ammunition.
Goody Wagon:	Catering trucks parked outside military bases to sell junk food to trainees and recruits.
Grab Ass:	Throwaway term for goofing around.
Grab or Hug the Belt:	North Vietnamese tactic of fighting close to U.S. forces to negate use of arty, close air support, etc.
Graves Registration:	Military unit assigned to handle dead personnel.
Grazing Fire:	Indirect fire to keep enemy forces pinned down, while friendly forces close in for decisive action.
Greased:	GI lingo for someone killed.
Grease Gun:	Korea: Tankers' weapon.
Green Door:	Popular name for NCO clubs
Green Machine:	Soldiers and Marines term for their respective service.
Green Wienie:	GI term for U.S. Army
Greeting:	Salutation at top of letter sent to draftees ordering them to report for induction into armed forces of the U.S.
Grenadier:	Vietnam, Korea II: Infantryman carrying an M-79 grenade launcher in lieu of an M-16 or M-60 machine gun.
Grenade Sump:	Pit dug (usually in a corner) to contain explosion from a grenade that landed in a foxhole, deliberately or accidently.
Ground Pounder:	Infantryman

Grunt:	USMC/Army term for foot soldier or infantryman.
Guard Duty:	Regular responsibility in the military.
Gun Bunny:	Vietnam, Korea II: Artilleryman.
Gunner:	USMC Warrant Officer.
Gunship:	Vietnam, Korea II: Helicopter armed with 20mm cannons, 40mm grenade launcher, 7.62 mini guns and "frag" with rockets. Aka cobra gunships.
Gun Trucks:	Vietnam: U.S. Army 5-ton vehicles armored with steel plating and heavily armed.
G -Sections:	General Staff Sections
	G-1 Personnel
	G-2 Intelligence
	G-3 Operations
	G-4 Logistics
	G-5 Civil Affairs

HOTEL

Hotel:	Eighth letter of phonetic alphabet.
Hack it:	As in can you hack it? Take the pressure?
Hairless Pussy:	Vulgarity about Asian females alleged lack of genitalia hair.
HALO:	Korean War: Airborne technique of paratroopers trained to jump at "High Altitude Low Opening."
Ham and Motherfuckers:	GI vulgarity for C-ration can of ham and beans.
Hamburger Hill:	Vietnam: Site of May 1969 battle in Ashau Valley; involved units of 101st AMD and ARVN units against dug-in North Vietnamese soldiers.
Hammocks;	Vietnam: Sleeping gear normally suspended between poles or trees.
Hand and Arm Signals:	see Hand Signals.
Hand Grenades:	Small, oval-shaped anti-personnel explosives, normally hurled at enemy personnel or positions. Seven NATO Code colors, with olive drab fragmentation grenades the most lethal.
Hang Fire:	Misfire of a weapon, often caused by wet or damaged ammunition.
Hanoi Hanna:	Vietnam: Nickname GIs gave to North Vietnamese female propaganda broadcaster.

Hanoi Herald:	USARV contemptuous term for *Pacific Stars & Stripes*. Military brass alleged anti-U.S. bias in reporting some U.S. Army units refused to seek out the enemy. Circa 1970.
Hanoi Hilton:	Vietnam: Aka Hoa Lo prison in North Vietnam; prison camp for captured USAF, USN, and USMC pilots.
Hanoi Jane:	Derogatory term applied to anti-war actress Jane Fonda; she visited North Vietnam in July 1972 and was photographed sitting on an anti-aircraft gun.
Hardcore:	Tough, single-minded, not easily intimidated.
Hardship Tour:	Vietnam, Korea II: Short or unaccompanied tour.
Hard Stripped:	U.S. Army NCO with the rank of buck sergeant or higher.
Hatchet Force:	Vietnam: U.S. Army Green Berets missions in South Vietnam, Cambodia and Laos, and North Vietnam.
Haul Ass:	Korean War: "Move out, right now!"
HAWK:	Korea II: Homing, All-Weather Killer missile; employed by 38th artillery brigade.
Hawk Patrols:	Vietnam: Units of 173rd AB Brigade.
Hazardous Duty Pay:	Vietnam, Korea II: EOD teams trained to find and dismantle bombs and booby traps.
Head:	Navy/USMC lingo for toilet.
Heads:	Vietnam: Regular drug users.

Headgear:	U.S. Army term for fatigue cap, garrison cap, overseas cap, saucer cap.
Head Honcho:	GI term for headman, boss, leader, supervisor.
Head Shed:	GI slang for headquarters of a military unit.
Heartbreak Ridge:	Korea: Major battle involving 2nd Inf. Div. and NPKA units. 3,700 U.S. casualties.
Heat Exhaustion:	Common affliction in humid war zones.
Heat Tabs:	Vietnam: Small blue chemical discs used by GIs to heat chow, etc.
HEET:	Vietnam: Rockets fired by Cobra gunships.
HE Fire:	Vietnam, Korea II: High Explosive round fired from M-79 grenade launcher.
Hell Fire Valley:	Korea: Nov. 1950 battle between CCP forces and British Royal Marines and U.S. Marines; significant casualties on both sides.
H-53 Helicopter:	USAF 88-foot-long Jolly Green Giant.
Helilifted:	Vietnam, Korea II: Using helicopters to insert/extract personnel and equipment.
Helmet:	Steel pot with liner. Little changed from WWII to Vietnam. Protective against shrapnel but not bullets.
Heroic American Killer:	Vietnam: Medal awarded to communist personnel for eliminating the enemy.

Hey Diddle Diddle, Straight up the Middle:	Korean War: Clever phrase indicating a forward movement.
Hide in our assholes:	Korea, Vietnam: Intense need to make oneself as inconspicuous as possible in the face of enemy fire.
High Crawl:	Infantry technique for moving toward an objective keeping medium low to the ground.
High Order:	Military term for explosion
Higher Echelon:	Higher ranking personnel.
Higher-Higher:	Those at the top of the chain of command.
H-Hour:	Decisive time to act.
H & I Fire:	Vietnam: Harassment and Interdiction fire. Artillery salvoes used to disrupt and demoralize enemy forces. Fired at all hours of day and night. Accounted for an estimated 95 percent of all arty fired.
Hill Fights:	Vietnam: Battles before North Vietnamese attack on Khe Sanh, near Camp Carroll, 1968.
Hip Deep in the Big Muddy:	From a Pete Seeger anti-Vietnam War song. Theme was that U.S. was involved in a quagmire of its own making.
Hi-Valu:	Vietnam: USAF term for technologically sophisticated equipment, but also for caskets carrying dead servicemen.
Hmong: Vietnam, Laos:	Indigenous people who allied with U.S. against communist forces.
Ho Chi Minh:	North Vietnamese leader, 1945-1969.

Ho Chi Manh Sandals:	Footwear worn by VC and sometimes NVA. Many made from strips of rubber.
Ho Chi Minh Trail Vietnam:	Series of trails from North Vietnam through Laos and Cambodia. Avenue for troops and supplies sent to fight U.S. and ARVN forces in South Vietnam.
Hog:	Vietnam, Korea II: Cobra gunships designed to carry rockets and miniguns for close air support of ground troops.
Hog:	Vietnam: Rocket-launching aerial artillery ship carrying 76 rockets.
Hoi Chanh Vietnam:	Viet Cong defectors.
Hold Baggage:	Amount of personal property a GI was allowed to ship from overseas to CONUS. The higher the rank the more pounds of hold baggage authorized to be shipped home.
Hollywood Wounds:	Vietnam: Minor wounds serious enough to get out of the field but not serious enough to cause permanent injury.
Holy Moses:	Korean War: Navy aircraft rockets.
Honest John Rockets:	Korea II: Rockets located near DMZ and designed to attack enemy aircraft.
Honey Buckets:	Korea, Vietnam, Korea II: GI term for collected human waste often used as fertilizer.
Hooch:	GI term for hut or house occupied by indigenous personnel.

Hooch Maids:	Vietnam: Indigenous females employed by the U.S. military to attend basic housekeeping needs of GIs.
You better HONK:	GI lingo meaning, "Get with it troop," or "damn right you'll follow my orders or else."
Horizontal Vaginas:	GI extrapolation about the imagined shape of Asian female genitalia; only feasible to very uninitiated.
Horn:	Vietnam, Korea II: RTO term for radio, often a PRC-25.
Hospital Folds:	Technique taught to trainees/recruits to fold bunk sheets in order to make corners uniformly tight.
Hospital Ships:	Korea, Vietnam: Naval vessels anchored off the coasts to care for wounded GIs.
Hostile Fire:	Lethal projectiles launched toward the enemy with intent to wound and kill and thus defeat opposing forces.
Hostile v. Non-Hostile Deaths:	Official categories for military deaths; sometimes a thin line between said designations.
Hour System:	U.S. military time system. Begins at zero 100 hours (0100) and ends at 24 hundred hours (2400). The 24 hours in a day thus delineated on a continuous basis.
House Boys:	Korea II: Indigenous males employed by the U.S. military to attend basic housekeeping needs of GIs; also pulled KP.

Hue:	Ancient capital of Vietnam; site of furious fighting during Tet Offensive in 1968.
Huey:	GI name for HU 1D Bell-manufactured helicopter made famous during Vietnam era and used for carrying troops and supplies. Later designated UH 2D; eight different models.
Human Chain Saw:	Vietnam: GI talk for clearing a Landing Zone ([Z) with a machete.
Human Remains Pouches:	Military term for body bags.
HUMINT:	Korean War: Human Intelligence Collection.
Hunter-Killer Patrols:	Korea II: Infantry tactics along DMZ.
Hunter-Killer Teams:	Vietnam: U.S. Army "Pink Teams" infiltrated into Cambodia and Laos.

INDIA

India:	Ninth letter of phonetic alphabet.
Ia Drang Valley:	Vietnam: Area near Laotian border; in October 1965 the U.S. 1st Air cav. fought a major battle against NVA troops.
I.B.:	Infantry Bars.
I can't hear you:	Phrase frequently heard during BCT and AIT indicating the cadre wasn't satisfied with the level of enthusiasm by GIs.
Ice Cream Parlor:	Korea II: MPs assigned to Joint Security Area (JSA) near Panmunjom description of a pink, tile-roofed NKPA guard shack erected in 1967.
Ice Cream Soldiers USMC:	Semi-derogatory term for Army personnel.
ICX:	Vietnam: Intelligence Coordination and Exploitation, circa 1967. Later called *Phuonq Huong* or Phoenix program of CIA.
I Corps, II Corps, III Corps, IV Corps:	Vietnam: U.S. military designation of war zones in South Vietnam-North to south.
I Corps (Gp):	Korea II: Described as largest combat deployed unit in the Free World. Consisted of two U.S. infantry divisions, four ROKA infantry divisions and one ROK Marine brigade.

If it's dead and it's
Vietnamese, it's
Viet Cong: Vietnam: Phrase used by some GIs to
                              indicate that the body count of enemy
                              dead trumped other criteria, including
                              differentiating between friend and foe.

If I say jump, you
say how high: Phrase encountered in training that
                              emphasized the need to follow orders
                              to a "T."

IG Inspector General.   In Air Force and Army the designated
                              ombudsman to insure redress outside
                              the chain of command.

IG Inspection: Regularly scheduled intense inspection
                              of personnel and equipment.

III MAF: Vietnam: Third Marine Amphibious
                              Force.

Illumination Rounds: Vietnam, Korea II: Artillery rounds
                              fired to expose enemy positions.

Imjin River: Major River separating parts of North
                              and South Korea; partially follows
                              the DMZ. ROKs call it "River of the
                              Dead."

Imjin Scouts: Korea II: Badge established by U.S.
                              Army in 1967 to reward soldiers
                              performing hazardous duty north of
                              the Imjin River along DMZ.

I'm so short l could crawl
under a snake's belly
And not touch him: A happy GI about to go home.

Immediate Action Drills: Korea II: Training to react quickly
                              to ambushes – particularly while in
                              military vehicles.

Inactivated: Military units closed down.

Incident:	EOD teams: A call for a suspected or actual presence of an explosive that presents a hazard to lives or operations.
Incoming Mail:	Korea, Vietnam, Korea II: Term for enemy ordnance directed at a position, often from mortars or artillery shells.
Indian Country:	Vietnam, Korea II: Enemy territory.
Indianhead:	Nickname for U.S. Army's 2nd Inf. Div.
Indian Howitzer:	Korea II: GI term for M-79 grenade launcher.
Infantry:	Foot soldiers and marines.
Infantry Training Regiment:	USMC advanced training.
In Min Gun:	North Korean military
Infiltrators:	Korea, Korea II: North Korean soldiers and spies sent into South Korea with the aim of creating an insurgency to overthrow the government.
In front of them all:	Korea II: Motto of U.S. Army Support Group near Panmunjom (DMZ).
International Operator:	Vietnam, Korea II: Conduit for telephone calls to CONUS.
Inghman Range:	Camp Casey, Korea: Touted as toughest marksmanship range in U.S. Army.
In/Out Processing:	Bureaucratic procedure of assigning and reassigning personnel.
Insert/Extract:	Deploying and recovering troops into a combat situation, often using helicopters.
Inspections:	Staple of military life. Senior NCOs and officers checking troops and equipment to insure high standards of efficiency and readiness.

Interlocking Fire:	Placement of weapons to insure that all areas of a potential enemy attack are covered.
In war, everything is realer than real:	Vietnam: U.S. Army doctor describing but not justifying military atrocities.
Iodine:	Ingredient in halazone tablets to purify water.
Iodine Purple Hearts:	Vietnam: USMC policy of reassigning out of country men with three purple hearts; problem was that some were for very minor wounds, barely scratches. Army policy to reassign wounded personnel to non-combat units in-country.
I.O.H.:	Vietnam: Imminence of hostility; tactical intelligence effort to predict enemy attacks.
IR:	Infared Scope. Developed by U.S. Army and predecessor to Starlight Scope that allowed a rifleman to detect enemy targets at night; illumination was provided by moon and stars.
Iron Detractors:	Korea II: Tanker's term for M-48 tank, a 52-ton behemoth.
Iron Triangle:	Korea: October 1952 battle involving CCP and U.5, Army divisions. Area included Jane Russell, White Horse and Pike's Peak battlegrounds.
I Spell:	Procedure for clarifying messages via radio/telephone in order to minimize mistakes using phonetic alphabet.

Insubordination:	Refers to lower ranking personnel who refused to follow orders issued by a superior officer.
It don't mean nothin':	Vietnam, Korea II: Fatalistic lament of GIs attempting to deal with day-to-day stress.
Ivymen Vietnam:	Members of 4th Inf. Div.

JULIO

Julio: Tenth letter of phonetic alphabet

Jamming: Attempt to interfere with enemy
                                communications. Generally two types:
                                (1) Spot (2) Barrage.

Jarhead: Semi-derogatory term for U.S. Marines

Jesus Nut: Connecting bolt that held the blades to
                                the frame of a Huey helicopter.

Jody: Mythical figure associated with BCT/
                                boot camp. The guy who stole your girl
                                while you were in the service.

Joe Chink: Korea, Korea II: GI term for Chinese
                                and North Korean soldiers.

John Waynes: Name of small can opener used by
                                Navy, Marines, and Coast Guard.

JSA: Korea II: Joint Security Area,

Judge Advocate
Claims Officer: Legal officer assigned to look out for
                                the interests of military personnel.

Juicers: Military personnel who preferred and
                                sometimes abused alcohol as opposed
                                to other drugs.

Jump Boots: Special footgear worn by paratroopers.

Jump in your shit: Threat used by several generations of drill
                                instructors/drill sergeants to instill fear in
                                recruits/trainees.

Jump Wings: Badge awarded to airborne-qualified
                                personnel after five tactical jumps.

Jungle Warfare School: U.S. Army training center in Panama
                                Canal Zone.

KILO

Kilo:	Eleventh letter of phonetic alphabet.
Ka-do:	Korean for "Get Away!"
Kaesong Corridor:	Korea II: Traditional invasion route from North Korea to Seoul, South Korea.
Kay Sickia:	Korean for "Son of a Bitch!"
K-Bar:	Famous knife used by Marines in Pacific Theater in WW II; also an Army version. Known for durability and adaptability; also used by troops in Korea and Vietnam.
Keep up the fire, sir:	Motto of 9rh Regt. of 2nd Inf. Div.
Kentucky Windage:	In marksmanship, correcting for physical conditions by aiming to a side of target rather than adjusting sights.
Kidnap Squads:	Terrorist tactic employed by Viet Cong in Vietnam and North Korean commandos along DMZ and in interior.
Khaki:	Tan-color uniforms normally worn by GIs in summer and while serving in tropical areas, especially in transit. Rarely used for day-to-day duty.
Khe Sanh:	Site of major North Korean attack against USMC base in northwest South Vietnam in 1968. Originally a U.S. Army Special Forces outpost.
Khe Sanh Red:	Vietnam: Severe dust pollution present in NW South Vietnam.
Khoung Khoung:	Vietnamese for "No, No!"

Kick ass and take names:	GI lingo for no nonsense approach to a situation.
Kill:	What combat trained soldiers and marines were taught was their prime military mission.
Kill Chuck:	Vietnam, GI lingo for killing Viet Cong.
Kill them and let God sort it out:	Vietnam: Idea that the mission is to eliminate the enemy and don't fret the details.
Killing Zone:	Typically the site of an ambush-area where most of lethal fire was directed and where most casualties were sustained.
Kimchee Cab, Squat, Cabinet:	Favorite Korean food incorporated into GI lingo to describe various aspects of Korean culture that seemed relevant in their lives. Also, "deep kimchee," meaning big trouble.
Kim Il Sung:	Founder of Communist North Korea, established in 1948. He launched the Korean War on 25 June 1950. Announced in late 1966 that he would unite North and South Korea under Communist rule by end of 1970. Lived Between 1912 and 1994.
Kim Il Sung Bridge:	Korean War: Bloody part of Heartbreak Ridge near Mundung-ni.
Kimpo Air Base:	Main air base and international airport near Seoul, South Korea.
Kiowa:	U.S. Army helicopter introduced in 1977.

Kit Carson Scouts:	Vietnam: Former Viet Cong who defected and volunteered to work as scouts for U.S. forces.
Klicks:	U.S. military metric system abbreviation for kilometers; used instead of miles.
Know your enemy:	Korea II: 19-day training course initiated by Maj. Roger Donlon of 2nd Inf. Div. in 1967 (Donlon won Medal of Honor in Vietnam in 1954).
Kontum:	Vietnam: Large city in Central Highlands. Site of many battles.
Korean War Units:	Under UNC, U.S. Army units included 2nd Inf. Div.3rd Inf. Div., 7th Inf. Div., 24th Inf. Div., 25th Inf. Div., 1st cav. Div., 40th Inf. Div., 45th Inf. Div. Also, 1st Marine Division, 5th USAF, and USN and Coast Guard ships. A total of 16 countries sent forces to Korea.
Korea Units 1966-1971:	Under direction of CINCUSARPAC, Fort Shafter, Hawaii: 8th Army, I Corps (Gp), I Corps Arty, 2nd Inf. Div.,7th Inf. Div., 38th Artillery Brigade, 4th Missile Command, KORSCOM, 8th Army Rear,314th Air Division under command of 5th Air Force, Naval and Marine advisory personnel. Also a company of Thai troops served.
KORSCOM:	Korea II: Korea Support Command; prior to 1970 it was designated FASCOM, with HQ near ASCOM City.
Korean Service Corps:	Korea II: Indigenous personnel used to assist allied units' logistical requirements.

| KP: | Kitchen Police: A staple of Army life. A drudgery-laden detail intensely disliked by most GIs. Often involved an 18-hour day of cleaning pots and pans, grease traps, waxing and buffing mess hall floors, etc. |
| Kupsa Edewa: | Korean for "Houseboy, come here!" |

LIMA

Lima:	Twelfth letter of phonetic alphabet.
Laager:	Vietnam, Korea II: Chopper base or overnight encampment for helicopters.
Lam Son 719:	Vietnam: Joint U.S. Army-ARVN, SV Marines offensive against NVA in Laos Feb-April 1971. Not successful.
Land of the Morning Calm:	Name for Korea.
Land Navigation:	Arriving at a military objective using maps, compasses, natural features, etc.
Land Line:	Telephone wires, aka Lima-Lima.
Lane Grader:	Instructor, normally in advanced training centers.
Lao Dong:	North Vietnamese Communist Party.
LAPS:	Vietnam: Low Altitude Parachute Supply.
Latrine:	Army and Air Force term for toilet.
Latrine Duty:	Korea, Vietnam, Korea II: Arduous detail that involved empting and disposing of large quantities of human waste. Often burned in 50-gallon barrels.
Latrine Types:	In the field: (1) Cat Hole (2) Straddle Trench (3) Deep Pit.
Latrine at Fort Polk, La:	Vietnam era: Always five rolls of toilet paper in barrack's latrine.
Laws of Land Warfare:	Rules allegedly followed by signers of Geneva Conventions to make combat as humane as possible.

Land of the Big PX:	GI term for U.S.
LAW:	Vietnam, Korea II: Light Anti-Tank Weapon. Fired once and then discarded.
Lay Dog:	Vietnam: Term used by LRRPs and Special Forces personnel to hide and avoid enemy contact.
LBE:	U.S. Army/USMC: Load Bearing Equipment.
LBJ:	Vietnam: GI term for Long Binh Jail the main incarceration stockade for miscreants, located near Saigon. Mocking reference to President Lyndon B, Johnson.
LC:	Vietnam: Line of Contact
LCU:	Korea II: Utility Landing Craft; assigned to U.S. Army's 104-ship fleet.
Leathernecks:	U.S. Marines.
Leatherneck Square:	Vietnam: 3rd Marine Division area of operation south of DMZ at Dong Ha.
Leg Unit:	Infantry troops as opposed to artillery, armor, airborne, Rangers, Special Forces, etc.
Let's move it:	Frequently used command directed at trainees/recruits.
Leisure Army:	Vietnam: Sarcastic term for service in the waning days of the war, with many remaining troops assigned to rear echelon, make-work jobs.
Lifer:	GI term-usually uncomplimentary-for career NCOs and officers.

Light:	Vietnam: Description of casualties on Hill 937 (Hamburger Hill battle in May 1969).
Light Bird:	Slang for lieutenant colonel.
Light 'em if you've got 'em':	OK given by leaders for men to smoke if so desired.
Lights Out:	Mandatory switching off lights in a barracks-normally about 2300 hours or 11 p.m.
Lima Charlie:	Vietnam, Korea II: Term used by RTOS to indicate "loud and clear."
Lines of Defense:	Vietnam, Korea II: (1) Perimeter (2) Barbed Wire (3) Claymores (4) Patrolling.
Line Kansas:	Korean War: Area of final push of UNC forces to secure as much territory as possible before the Armistice.
Line Papa:	Korea II: Defensive positions south of Han River near Seoul designed to halt an all-out North Korean attack.
Litter Racks:	Vietnam, Korea II: Chopper load of wounded with most serious cases on bottom racks.
Little Bears:	Vietnam: A Co. 25th Aviation Bn. 25th Inf. Div. Used Delta-model Hueys.
Little Green Chair:	Punishment employed at Fort Polk, La. and other AIT centers to discipline fire team leaders. Consisted of being forced to crouch against a wall in a sitting position with arms outstretched and forced to remain in that position indefinitely.

Lister Bag:	Large container transported by truck or dropped into the field by aircraft to supply potable water or other liquids to troops.
Listen Up:	Term widely used during Vietnam era meaning, "Give me your undivided attention and now!"
Little Chicago:	Korea II: 7th Inf. Div. artillery range near Camp Casey.
Live Fire Exercise:	Shooting live ammunition in training, as opposed to firing blanks.
Loach:	Vietnam: Small U.S. Army helicopter used for reconnaissance.
LOC:	Line of Communication
Lock and Load:	Term for loading a magazine into rifle but keeping selector switch on safe.
Log Day:	Vietnam: Temporary stand-down in the field, when hot food, mail, etc. were delivered.
Long Binh:	Vietnam: City near Saigon that served as headquarters for MACV.
Long Handles:	Korea I: Marine term for long johns.
Long John:	Vietnam, Korea II: Long antennae that was optional for use on PRC-25 radio provided greater range.
Long Noses:	Asian view of facial characteristics of Caucasian military personnel.
Long Shadows:	Vietnam: Tall Caucasian soldiers located in Laos (circa 1970) and believed to be military defectors.
Long Toms:	U.S. Army 175mm artillery pieces.

Lost city of the DMZ:	Changdan, South Korea: once contained a population of 69,000; abandoned during Korea n War.
Loud and Clear:	Radio/Telephone system: Indication that communication transmission was understood. See Lima Charlie.
Low Crawl:	Technique taught to trainees/recruits that consisted of lying on the stomach and moving forward along the ground propelled by elbows and knees. Very exhausting.
Low Quarters:	Military term for black shoes worn with Class A uniforms.
LRPs:	Vietnam: U.S. Army: Long Range Reconnaissance Patrols.
LRP Motto:	"All for one and one for all."
LRRPs:	Vietnam: Long Range Reconnaissance Patrols. Extra "R" indicated teams more oriented toward reconnaissance as opposed to seeking to inflict enemy casualties.
Luke the Gook:	Korea, Vietnam: Term for indigenous enemy forces, mostly derogatory.
LURPs:	Vietnam: Dried rations packed in plastic bags-some freeze-dried and carried by tactical units.
Luster Leader Control:	Korea II: Code name for commander of a field unit.
LT (el tee):	Abbreviation for a lieutenant often serving as a platoon leader.
LZ:	Vietnam, Korea II: Landing Zone.

MIKE

Mike:	Thirteenth letter of phonetic alphabet.
MAC:	Military Airlift Command. USAF planes used to transport GIs to overseas assignments. Also carried wounded and deceased GIs to CONUS. Civilian airlines also used.
MACV:	Military Assistance Command, Vietnam.
MACV-SOG:	Military Assistance Command and Studies and Observation Group. More accurately Special Operations Group.
Mad Minute:	Vietnam: GIs firing weapons en masse to discourage enemy activity.
Mae Bong:	Korean term for "Bird Mountain." Site of highest HAWK missile base in the world. Elevation 4,750 feet and 17 miles south of DMZ. Enemy positions visible on a clear day.
MAF:	Vietnam: Marine Amphibious Force.
Maggot Wagon:	See Goody Wagon
Make your buddy smile:	Phrase used by some drill instructors to encourage GIs to squeeze together in so called "cattle trucks" so all personnel could fit in.
Malaysian Fan Method:	Technique for patrolling in a systematic fashion.
Mail Call:	A favorite diversion for GIs-letters and packages from home.
Main Force:	Vietnam: Large Viet Cong units of company to battalion size, mainly operating in Mekong Delta region.

Malingering:	Term for goldbricking or finding an excuse for not performing assigned duty.
Malaria Control Pills:	Vietnam, Korea II: Issued to GIs-mainly chloroquine, primiquin, quinine.
Mama San:	Korean War: GI term for indigenous female personnel; borrowed from Japanese word for an adult woman.
Mang Ho:	Vietnam: Vietnamese for "Brave Tiger." Viet Cong name for ROK troops.
MAP:	Military Assistance Program: U.S. aid to anti-Communist regimes in Asia.
Map:	Detailed topographical representation of terrain broken down into grids. GIs taught to read "right and up."
Marble Mountain:	Vietnam: Air facility south of Da Nang
Marksman:	The lowest of three ratings of shooting efficiency.
Mark Time:	Soldiers marching in place before receiving the command to move forward.
Marmite Cans:	Korea I: Large canisters used to drop food and water to troops in the field.
MARS:	Military Affiliate Radio System. Calls from overseas relayed by short wave radio to stateside telephone numbers.
Marine A4s:	Vietnam: USMC tactical jets.
Marine Corps:	Branch of U.S. military founded in 1775. Known for distinguished emblem of globe, anchor and eagle. Motto: *Semper Fidelis* (Always Faithful). Known for tenacity and courage.

Marine Corps Creed:	"My rifle is my life."
Marine Force Logistics Command:	FLC
MASH:	Korea I: Mobile Army Surgical Hospital. Deployed in Korea until 1990. 43rd in country 1969-1971. Last unit deployed outside Korea inactivated in 2005.
Massacre Valley:	Korea I: USMC term for area around Hoeng-song that saw large U.S. Army casualties in February 1951.
Master Blaster:	U.S. Army airborne soldier with at least 100 static line jumps to his credit.
MAT:	Vietnam: Mobile Advisory Team; unit normally comprised of two officers, two EMs and one interpreter.
Maternity Dress:	Jocular reference to U.S. Army jungle fatigue jacket worn outside trousers that from a certain vantage point on a heavy soldier resembled a pregnant woman's garb.
Mayday:	International call for help.
Meal Card:	Small card issued to military personnel for use in mess halls; often had to be displayed before being admitted.
Measle Maps:	Korea II: Wall maps used by 8tn Army Commanding General Charles H. Bonesteele III to keep track of enemy activity. Black dots indicated North Korean infiltrators; red dots indicated fire fights. Circa 1967-1968.
McGuire Rig:	Vietnam: Nylon sling attached to a 120-foot rope and dropped from a helicopter; used to extract personnel from hazardous situations.

MEB:	Marine Expeditionary Brigade
Mechanized:	U.S. Army units that primarily used vehicles for operations.
MedCap:	Vietnam, Korea II: Medical units assisting the local population (winning hearts and minds).
Medic:	U.S. Army medical personnel often assigned to the field to provide first aid for wounded soldiers.
MDM:	Movement for a Democratic Military. A USMC officer-created anti-Vietnam War movement centered at Camp Pendleton, CA.
Meat Grinder:	Cambodia: Tactics employed by Khmer Rouge and NVA to inflict demoralizing casualties on the fragile Cambodian government and military. Idea was to employ hit and run tactics.
Meet the Phantom:	Vietnam: GI saying: "If you go too many times into the night, you will meet the phantom." Meaning that if you push your luck you could get killed.
Me-Guk:	Korean term for Americans.
Melidosis:	Vietnam: Bacterial disease labeled a "time bomb" for certain afflicted GIs.
Men with painted faces:	Vietnam: Enemy term for LRRPs and Special Forces personnel wearing grease-paint camouflage on the skin.
Messages:	(1) Flash (2) Immediate (3) Priority (4) Routine.
Meter:	Standard military metric measurement. One meter equals 39.37 inches.
Meter-Meter:	Korean version of "Look-Look."

Mere Gook Rule:	Vietnam era: Idea that lives of indigenous personnel were less valuable than American lives.
Methods of Search:	(1) Preservative (2) Systematic (3) Observation.
Mess Duty:	Navy and USMC term for KP.
Mickey Mouse Boots:	Korea II: Heavy overshoes worn in frigid weather conditions.
Mickey Mouse Rules:	Catch-all phrase to describe onerous and often illogical rules and regulations imposed on lower echelon troops by higher ups. Considered a form of discipline.
MiG Alley:	Korea I: Area adjacent to Yellow Sea between North Korea and Communist China; site of many air battles between allied and enemy forces between 1950 and 1955.
MiG:	Korea, Vietnam, Korea II: Soviet designed fighter jets used by Communist forces. Most famous were the MiG-15s, MiG-17s, MiG-19s, and MiG-21s.
Mike Pappas:	Military Police.
MI:	Military Intelligence; some wags joke that it is an oxymoron.
MIAs:	Missing in Action. Service members who vanished in a battle or mission and were never seen again. 7,500 from Korea and 2,200 from Vietnam. Small number from Korea II.
Military Bearing:	Looking and acting like a disciplined member of the U.S. armed forces.

Military Courtesy:	The practice of member of a hierarchical organization to extend respect to those of a higher rank by saluting, following orders, etc.
Military Police:	See MP.
Military Pride:	Vietnam: Senator Ted Kennedy's accusation against commander of 101st AMD who ordered assault on Hamburger Hill in May 1969.
Military Uniforms:	(1) Duty (2) Work (3) Dress.
Mine Detector:	Long-handled electronic instrument designed to find lethal explosions planted in roads, trails, etc.
Minefields:	Categorized: (1) Protective (2) Defensive (3) Barrier (4) Nuisance (5) Phony.
Mines and Boobv Trap School:	Vietnam: Integral to anti-guerrilla training in 25th Inf. Div.
Miss Fire:	Weapon that fails to fire properly; often the result of faulty ammunition or dirty weapons.
Mission of the Infantry:	Close with and destroy the enemy.
Mine Card:	Vietnam, Korea II: Illustrated card issued to troops detailing various antipersonnel and anti-vehicle mines used by both friendly and enemy forces. Also how to recognize a minefield.
Minju Chosen:	North Korea: Official government newspaper.
Mister:	U.S. Navy, USMC, U.S. Coast Guard address to an officer with the rank of lieutenant. Also term for Army warrant officer.

Mobile Ambush:	Vietnam: USMC lingo for all-volunteer ambush units.
Mobile Guerrilla Forces:	South Vietnamese Militia.
Mod Wrist Band:	Vietnam, Korea II: wide, usually black, leather watch band worn by many GIs.
Model Defensive Village:	Korea II: South Korean villages singled out to defend against Communist subversion.
Mojave:	Vietnam: CH-37 helicopter used for supply missions.
Mongolian Piss-Cutter:	Korea I: Fur-lined cap worn by GIs.
Monkey Mountain:	Vietnam: Area nine miles northeast of Da Nang AB.
Monsoon:	Weather pattern prominent in Asia in summer and winter. Often characterized by heavy rains and typhoons.
Monster:	Vietnam: Numerous Claymore mines strung together to create one huge explosion.
Monuron:	Dioxin used in Vietnam and Korean DMZ.
Morale:	An intangible, subjective sense of esprit de corps among the troops. Difficult to measure and constantly fluctuating.
Moratorium Days:	Vietnam era: Massive anti-war demonstrations on 15 Oct. and 15 Nov 1969.
Morning Report:	Paperwork required of every military unit detailing the number of personnel available for duty, and the status of those not available.

Morphine Surete:	Device carried by medics and corpsmen to inject a painkiller into a severely wounded soldier/marine.
Moose Maintenance System:	Korea I, Korea II: GI term for girlfriends, who were often a conduit to black market activities.
MOS:	Military Occupational Specialty. The serviceman's job. During Vietnam era the U.S. Army had more than 150 occupational specialties.
Moskosi:	Korea I, Korea II: Japanese term for "little" adopted by GIs, now in civilian vernacular.
Most Riki-Tick:	Vietnam: GI term for "soon" or "quick."
Most Tick:	Korea II: GI term for "pretty soon."
Mother's Day (Battle of):	Vietnam: May 1967; involved 1st Bn 327th Inf. 101st AMD.
Motor Pool:	Military element responsible for maintain vehicles such as jeeps, trucks, sedans, etc.
Move Mission:	Korea II: Tanks maintained to optimal combat-ready status.
MP:	Military Police. See Mike Papas.
MPC:	See Funny Money.
MP Roving Patrols:	Korea II: KORSCOM'S 142nd MP Co. Focused on patrols around Taegu and Pusan.
MRF:	Vietnam: Mobile Riverine Force.
MSR:	Vietnam: Main Supply Route.

MSA:	Military Security Agency. Units often in charge of exterior security at large bases. Some areas patrolled by sentry dog handlers.
MSTS:	Military Sea Transportation Service (ship).
Mud Oven:	Cooking pit dug by GIs in the field.
MUST:	Korea I: Military Unit Self-Contained Transportation.
Muster Formation:	Bringing elements of a unit together.
Musumi:	Korea I: Japanese term for girl. GIs coined term "moose" to describe a girlfriend.
M-14:	Standard infantry rifle used by U.S. forces from late 1950s to late 1960s.
M-16:	Lightweight automatic rifle used during Vietnam era. Fired a 5.56mm round from a 20-30 round magazine. Could be fired single shot, semi, or automatic.
M-17 Decontaminating and Reimpregnating Kit:	Equipment issued along with gas mask to counter effects of chemical or biological attack.
M4T6:	Pontoon Bridge-one of largest pieces of tactical equipment used by U.S. Army.
M-48:	Vietnam, Korea II: Main battle tank.
M-60:	Vietnam, Korea II: Machine-gun that fired 7.62mm NATO rounds and weighed 25 pounds.
M-60 (Tank):	Vietnam, Korea II: Main battle tank replaced M-48 in early 1970s.
M-79:	See grenade launcher.

M442:	U.S. Army flamethrower system deployed as a 190-gallon tank mounted on a five-ton truck.
M151:	Vietnam era jeep. 600 pounds lighter than predecessor M38A1, but with more power.
M108/109:	Nomenclature for a howitzer artillery piece.
MS51:	Korea I, Vietnam: Sheridan tank.

NOVEMBER

November:	Fourteenth letter of phonetic alphabet.
NCO:	Noncommissioned Officer. Enlisted personnel with rank of E-5 to E-9. Top Army NCO is Command Sergeant Major of the Army.
NCIS:	Naval Criminal Investigative Service.
N DP:	Korea I, Vietnam, Korea II: Night Defensive Position.
Need to know:	Military principle indicating that classified information was restricted to the mission at hand; only personnel directly involved were privy to it.
Negative Friendly Casualties:	Situation report indicating no personnel were wounded or killed in a particular action.
Neutralize:	Vietnam, Korea II: U.S. Army term for killing the enemy.
New Action Army:	Vietnam era: Recruiting slogan for U.S. Army.
NG:	National Guard.
NI:	Nixon's Island; GI term for CONUS.
Nice talk, GI:	Term of jest about another GI using negative language about someone or something.
Night Barrier Commander:	Korea II: Officer in charge of a unit assigned to DMZ.
Night darker than a whore's heart:	Korean War profanity.

Night Halt:	Vietnam: Similar to NDP. A unit in the field finding a secure area to spend the night.
Night Laager Site:	See Laager site.
Nightmare Range:	Korea II: Area near Camp Red Cloud. Site of massive ordnance expenditures in coordinated training involving Air Force and Army units. Sometimes described as "Where all hell broke loose."
Ninety:	Vietnam: 90mm shoulder-fired recoilless rifle; used by NVA and Main Force VC.
Ninety Day Wonder:	Derogatory name for Officer Candidate School graduate; commissioned as a 2nd lieutenant in U.S. Army Reserves.
Ninth Infantry Division:	Vietnam: Nickname "Old Reliables" In-country 1966-1969.
Nixon's order to Gen Creighton Abrams on 21June 1969:	"Conduct this war with a minimum of American casualties."
NKs:	North Koreans.
No Gun Ri:	Korea I: Site of massacre of civilians by U.S. troops in July 1950. Dozens to 500 killed.
No Contact:	Vietnam: Uneventful mission
No Man's Land:	Korea II: GI term for DMZ.
Non-Hostile:	Military categorization of casualties due to other than hostile causes.

No Slack:	As in "he's cutting me no slack," meaning no leeway or diverging from set rules or procedures.
Nonspecific Urethritis:	Medical term for The Clap, or gonorrhea. A malady that afflicted a significant number of GIs during the Vietnam era.
NST:	No Sooner Than.
Not sentimental, but semi-mental:	GI put-down.
Numbah Ten:	Vietnam, Korea II: Indigenous personnel's rating of some GI's actions, and vice versa.
No Sweateda GI:	Korea II: Pidgin English used by some indigenous personnel. Meaning "Go for it."
Nungs:	Vietnam: Chinese troops drawn from Highlands of South Vietnam.
Nouc Nam:	Vietnam: Foul smelling fish sauce consumed as a staple of Vietnamese diet.
NVA:	North Vietnamese Army
No walking wounded:	Vietnam, Korea II: What the projectile from an M-16 rifle was supposed to accomplish against enemy personnel.

OSCAR

Oscar:	Fifteenth letter of phonetic alphabet.
Oakland Army Depot:	Vietnam: Debarkation/Embarkation site for U.S. Army troops early in the war; later shifted to Fort Lewis, WA.
O.B Vietnam:	Order of Battle; tactical intelligence effort to predict enemy attacks.
Oceanside, California:	Area near Camp Pendleton. Destination for recruits headed to USMC boot camp.
OCS:	Officer Candidate School. An intense six-month training regimen for men qualified to earn rank of 2nd Lieutenant in Army Reserves.
OD Bandages:	Vietnam: Cloth bandages in first aid kits and adapted by GIs as head protection against sun, insects, etc.
OD:	Officer of the Day. Officer responsible for seeing that necessary details were performed after regular duty hours.
OD Wienie:	See Green Wienie
OER:	Officer Efficiency Report. A monthly evaluation of each officer by his superiors,
Off Duty:	Time for rest and relaxation.
Off Limits:	Area outside a military base not to be patronized by GIs-usually for sanitary, security or disciplinary reasons.
Office Hours:	USMC equivalent of non-judicial punishment.

Officer (s):	Upper echelon of chain of command. Officers graduating from West Point are commissioned; those who graduate from OCS and ROTC hold a reserve officer commission. Lowest rank is 2nd lieutenant; highest current rank is 4-star general. O-1 through 0-10.
Officer entering mess hall:	First GI to see him shouts, "At Ease."
Officer entering barracks:	First GI to see him shouts, "Attention!"
Olive Drab:	Dark brown/green color pattern in most Army/Marine uniforms and equipment. Various shades used from WW II through Vietnam era.
Olive green death machine:	Lingo for U.S. Army Cobra gunship
Old Man:	Nickname for Commanding Officer.
One Million Candle Parachute Flares:	Korean War: Capable of illuminating one square mile of land below.
One Ninety Third Brigade (193rd):	U.S. Army unit stationed in Panama Canal Zone during Vietnam era. Site of jungle warfare school.
On the Parallel:	38th parallel area that separated North and South Korea.
On Report:	Discipline imposed on lower ranking enlisted men judged guilty of some infraction, and thus subject to various degrees of punishment.
On your feet:	Order for GIs to jump to attention, normally in a training environment.
Opconned:	Operational Control; temporary assignment to another unit.

Open Ranks Inspection: Personnel, often a platoon, lined up in four rows, one behind the other and spaced for a thorough inspection of men and equipment.

Operational Mission: Korea II: USAF F-106 Delta Dart tactics.

Operation Carenton
I & II: Vietnam: March-April 1968 battles involving 3rd Bde. of 101st AMD v. NVA forces.

Operation Crazy Horse: Vietnam: March 1967, involving 1st Air Cav Operation Delaware: Vietnam: 1969, 101st AMD exercise in A Shau Valley.

Operation Dewey
Canyon II: See Lam Son 219. U.S. Army designation.

Operation Dewey
Canyon III: Vietnam: Anti-war rally held in Washington D.C. in April 1971.

Operation Farmgate: Vietnam: U.S. Navy Desoto patrols against North Vietnam; began in December 1962. Objective was to support South Vietnamese counterinsurgency forces.

Operation Fast Pace: Korea II: Planned redeployment of U.S. forces in anticipation of a large-scale North Korean attack in June 1970.

Operation Geronimo I: Vietnam: Offensive actions by U.S. Army units around Tuy Hoa, 1956-1967.

Operation Market Time: Vietnam: USN Swift Boat mission near Cua Viet, 8 miles south of DMZ in October 1967.

Operation Nevada Eagle: Vietnam: Involved units of 101st AMD in May 1968.

Operation Niagara: Vietnam: B-52 carpet bombing missions during Khe Sanh siege, 1968.

Operation Pegasus: Vietnam: U.S. Army 30,000-man relief force that arrived at Khe Sanh at end of siege, 1968.

Operation Pile Driver: Korea I: May 1951 I Corps offensive with objective of seizing the Iron Triangle.

Operation Ranch Hand: Vietnam: (USAF): Spraying Agent Orange over six million acres of South Vietnam 1962 and 1971.

Operation Ripcord: Vietnam: Involved units of 101st AMD against large NVA force in 1970.

Operation Ripper: Korea I: March 1.951 battle between 25th Inf. Div. and CCF; massive arty exchange killed over a thousand Chinese soldiers.

Operation Seafloat: Vietnam: U.S. and South Vietnamese navies mobile support base in Cua Lon River. Joint forces composed of swift boats, river assault craft, yabuta junks, and sea wolf helicopters. Also involved Vietnamese hospital ship, Vietnamese SEALS, RF/RP troops. On shore designated "solid anchor."

Operations Sergeant: Vietnam: NCO responsible to coordinate activities of LRPS in the field.

Operation Tomahawk: Korea I: March 1951 involving units of 187th Airborne combat Team against CCP troops near Munsan, South Korea.

Operation Vernon Lake II:	Vietnam: 1st Inf. Div. offensive in Feb. 1959.
OPLON:	U.S. Army Operation Control.
Orderly Room:	Main office of a company commander-normally under supervision of a first sergeant.
ORP:	Vietnam: Objective Rallying Point. A predetermined location for tactical forces to assemble when mission completed.
Osan, AB:	Korea II: USAF base; Agent Orange sprayed a round base 1970-1973.
Other war in Asia:	Korea II: 1966-1971
O Three Hundred (0300):	USMC MOS for infantryman.
Out:	Term for ending a RTO conversation.
Out Process:	Procedure for separation from U.S. military.
Out there in front of them all:	Korea II: MPs term for manning the "Bridge of No Return" near Panmunjom.
Out Geeing the G:	Vietnam: Term coined by Colonel David Hackworth of 9th Inf. Div. Idea to train his men to defeat Viet Cong guerrillas at their own game.
Over Flight:	Vietnam: Helicopters used to reconnoiter potential AOs.
Over here in the 'Nam':	Vietnam: GI phrase describing real life conditions.

Overseas Bars:	U.S. Army and USMC: hash marks worn on sleeves of dress uniform; one awarded for every six months of overseas duty in a war zone.
Over the hill:	Going AWOL or deserting a post or unit.
Overseas Telephone & Telegraph Service:	Connected GIs with stateside numbers.
Overhead Cover:	Korea I, Vietnam, Korea II: Utilization of heavy logs, sandbags, etc. to protect a bunker or foxhole from enemy fire, often camouflaged.
One Zero, One-One, One-Two, One-Three:	Vietnam, Korea II: Designation for members of a Green Beret or Special Forces A Team. Southeast Asia theater forces dispatched into Cambodia and Laos. In Korea, used in interior of South Korea to track North Korean commandos.

PAPA

Papa:	Sixteenth letter of phonetic alphabet.
PACEX:	Vietnam era; Pacific Commissary Exchange. Headquartered in Tokyo; provided a catalogue available to GIs to order tax-free merchandise.
Pace Setter:	Infantry unit: soldier who moved 4-10 meters ahead of a column to set rate of March.
PACEF:	Pacific Air Force; employed C-130 Hercules and C-141 Starlifter aircraft.
Package:	Vietnam: Tactic of employing helicopters of 101st AMD to recon areas near Quang Tri Province. In late 1969 101st replaced by 5th Mechanized Infantry Bde.
Papa San:	Japanese-derived term for an adult male. Used regularly by GIs in Asia.
Parade Rest:	Military formation: Soldiers remained in ranks but could relax and talk quietly.
PARAC:	Korea II; USAF Pacific Aerospace Rescue and Recovery Center, Osan AB.
Paraonimiasis Asia:	Parasite found in polluted waters.
Pararescue:	USAF: Airmen trained to rescue downed pilots.
Paratroopers:	Soldiers/marines/airmen trained to make tactical jumps from aircraft; considered elite troops.
Parris Island:	USMC Recruit Training Base in South Carolina.

Parrot's Beak:	Vietnam: Area about 40 miles northwest of Saigon near the Cambodia border; site of much enemy activity.
Passive Security:	Opposite of Active Security.
Password/Challenge:	See Challenge.
Pathfinders:	Vietnam: Paratroopers trained to secure a landing zone. Also called "Black Hats."
Patrol Base:	Geographical origination of a unit sent in a tactical operation.
Patrols:	Small units, normally squads or platoon sent to the field on reconnaissance and sometimes com bat operations.
Patrol Orders:	Instructions normally comprised of five paragraphs: (1) Situation (2) Mission (3) Execution (4) Admin & Logistics (5) Command & Signals.
PAVN:	People's Army of Vietnam (North)
Patches:	Mainly U.S. Army. Distinctive identification designs worn on uniforms. Ex: 1st Inf. Div. shoulder patch was a "Big Red One." Marines discontinued shoulder patches after WW II.
PBR:	Vietnam: Patrol River Boat. Armed fiberglass boats assigned to coastal waters in and around Mekong Delta.
PCPT:	Physical Combat Proficiency Test required of all combat troops in training.

Peace-loving, American-killing emulator:	Vietnam: Highest award to VC soldier who shot down a U.S. helicopter. The soldier received a month's leave, a watch, a ball-point pen and a bicycle.
P.D.:	Point Detonated Round-artillery shell that explodes on impact.
PDF:	Vietnam: Principle Direction of Fire.
PDQ:	Pretty Damn Quick!
Peaceon Ridge:	Fort Polk, La: Area of intensive infantry training.
People Sniffer:	Vietnam, Korea II: U.S. Army chemical device used to detect the presence of enemy personnel.
Perimeter Guards:	Security personnel who manned posts ranging from gates to bunkers, towers, etc. Manned 24 hours a day.
Permanent Party:	Cadre assigned to a unit for an extended tour.
Personnel Control Facility:	Location where AWOLs and deserters were returned to military custody.
Peter Meter:	Vulgarity as in "Take out your peter meter and check the angle of the dangle."
Peter Pilot:	Vietnam, Korea II: Copilot of a helicopter.
PFC:	U.S. Army/USMC: Private First Class. Vulgarity: private fucking civilian.
Phoenix Program:	Vietnam: CIA-directed effort to eliminate Viet Cong infrastructure in the South from 1967-1969. Reportedly, more than 81,000 killed.

Phonetic Alphabet:	NATO-sanctioned system of using words instead of letters to minimize miscommunications while relaying messages via radio/telephone.
Psychological Operations Officer:	Vietnam: Specifically, officer assigned to assist GIs with psychological problems.
Pi:	Vietnamese currency. Short for piaster.
Picto Map:	Vietnam: Photo of terrain taken from the air.
PIG:	Vietnam, Korea II: GI term for M-60 machine-gun.
PIGs:	GI derogatory term for MPs.
Pile On:	Vietnam:9th Inf. Div. tactic of surrounding and overwhelming an enemy force.
Pineapples:	Vietnam, Korea II: GI term for hand grenades.
Pinkville:	Vietnam: Aka My Lai (massacre).
Piss and Moan:	GI gripping.
Piss Tube:	Korea, Vietnam, Korea II: makeshift urinals used as latrines.
Plant a size 12 up your ass:	Generic training threat.
Platoon:	Army, Marines: Basic tactical unit. Normally under command of a platoon leader and platoon sergeant. Often consisting of four squads and/or a weapons section.

Platoon War:	Vietnam: Term used by Maj. Gen. Melvin Zais of 101st AMD to describe tactics of war. (Not a General's War as in WW II).
Platoon, company, forward march:	Moving a body of soldiers as a group for some objective.
PJs:	See USAF Pararescues.
Plantation Road:	Vietnam: Saigon vice area.
Plexiglass Stomach:	Semi-obscenity: "GI, you need a plexiglass stomach to see where you're going with your head up your ass."
P LF:	Paratroopers: Parachute Landing Fall. Technique taught to minimize injuries upon hitting the ground.
PME:	USAF: Professional Military Education.
Police the area:	See "Elbows and Asses."
Politics:	GI gripe about rules, regulations and perceived favoritism.
Point:	Korea I, Vietnam, Korea II: First man moving forward in a tactical situation. Considered very dangerous due to vulnerability to ambushes, booby traps, etc.
Poncho:	Plastic garment carried by GIs and worn during ran and other inclement weather.
Poontang:	GI vulgarity for sexual intercourse
Port Call:	Official orders cut directing personnel to report for overseas duty.
Potato Masher Grenades:	Korea I: GI term for North Korean grenades.

Porous Warfare:	Korea II: Enemy tactic of infiltration utilizing maximum dispersion and mobility. Term coined by 8th Army Commander Gen. Bonesteele.
PPC Japan:	Vietnam, Korea II: Source of instructional material and cards for U.S. military personnel.
Present Arms:	Act performed as part of manual of arms. Soldier held rifle directly in front in a vertical position.
Prick 25:	Vietnam, Korea II: GI term for field radio carried by RTO. Succeeded PRC-10.
Prime Beef:	Vietnam: Anti-war term for draftees. Korea II: USAF Prime Base Emergency Forces.
Principles of Patrolling:	(1) Sound organization (2) Situation (3) Inspections & Rehearsals (4) Economy of force (5) Security (6) Search and Attack.
Principles of Tracking:	(1) Displacement (2) Staining (3) Littering (4) Weathering.
Prisoners:	See Five S's.
Probe for a mine:	GIs trained to "look," "feel," "probe," "move." Often utilizing a bayonet.
Professional Recon Unit:	Vietnam: ARVN special forces.
Promotion Board:	Composed of a small group of senior NCOs to interview and evaluate enlisted men eligible for advancement in rank.
Profile:	Medical condition or injury that allowed some GIs to get reassigned out of the field.

Protective Reaction:	Vietnam: Policy of Nixon administration enacted in June 1969 to minimize offensive actions by U.S. combat troops; idea to lower casualties as U.S. forces began to withdraw.
Provost Marshal:	Unit responsible for enforcing military law.
P. S. Monthly:	U.S. Army: Preventive Maintenance Monthly magazine. Distributed to logistical, transportation, maintenance personnel. Motto: "We have the world's best equipment-take care of it."
PSP:	Vietnam: Perforated steel plating used as infrastructure foundations.
PT:	Physical Training. Important component of shaping a first-rate military man.
P 38:	Small, Army-designed can opener that came with a C-ration box. A tool that could also be used as a screwdriver.
Psywarriors:	Korean War: U.S. Army psychological warfare specialists.
Pucker Factor:	GI term for fear extreme enough to potentially affect bodily functions.
Puff the Magic Dragon:	Vietnam: USAF aircraft equipped with multiple guns and cannons; designed to provide air support for ground troops.
Pugil Sticks:	Padded poles used by trainees/recruits in training to stimulate aggression without causing harm to one's opponent. Normally one on one.
Puk Chin:	Korean for "Go North!"
Puking Buzzard:	Vietnam: GI slang for 101st AMD.

Pull Head Count:	Vietnam, Korea II: Detail involved checking meal cards of GIs entering mess hall.
Pull Rank:	Tried and true military tradition of higher ranking personnel imposing their authority on lower ranking personnel.
Punchbowl:	Korean War: Marine name for extinct volcanic crater near 38th parallel; scene of heavy fighting in 1953.
Punji Stakes/Sticks/Pits:	Vietnam, Korea II: Sharpened bamboo weapons placed by Viet Cong and North Koreans to intimidate the enemy. Often smeared with human excrement to increase chance of infection.
Pup Tents:	Small shelters; usually one half carried by one soldier; used for bivouac conditions.
Purple Heart:	High decoration awarded to service members killed or wounded in action.
Purple Heart Hill:	Vietnam: Area near Chu Lai; scene of numerous enemy attacks.
Pussy Whipped:	Vulgarity to describe a GI who allowed his hormones to rule his head.
Put all the food in your mouth and chew it outside:	BCT: Mocking harassment of soldiers by cadre to intimidate them into consuming chow as fast as possible in order to allow others access to the mess hall.
Put the hurt on you:	Generic training threat.
PX:	Post Exchange. Building set aside for GIs to shop for personal and military items. Most items tax-free.

Pyongyang Polly: Korea II: GI nickname for female North Korean propagandist who broadcast to U.S. and ROK forces.

PZ: Vietnam, Korea II: Pickup zone.

QUEBEC

Quebec:	Seventeenth letter of phonetic alphabet.
QCS:	Vietnam: Elite South Vietnamese police; accused by some of harassing and/or robbing and assaulting GIs.
Quad.50:	Vietnam: Four .50 cal. machine-guns mounted on a vehicle.
Quangtri Combat Base:	Vietnam: Located some 19 mile south of 17th parallel in northern South Vietnam. Home of USMC 3rd Div. 1966-1969. Later home of Army's 1st Bde. 5th Mechanized Inf. Div. from 1969-1971.
Queen of Battle:	The Infantry.
Queers in the Rear:	Combat troops' derogatory term for support troops.
Quick Kill Method:	Shooting technique taught in BCT. Premised on instinctive reaction rather than rifle sights to aim and fire at an enemy.
Quick Time:	Army/USMC: Moving out on the double.
Quonset Hut:	Korea I, Vietnam, Korea II: Prefabricated buildings used to house offices, supplies, barracks, etc.

ROMEO

Romeo:	Eighteenth letter of phonetic alphabet.
RA:	Regular Army. Derogatory: "Regular Assholes."
Rabbit:	Vietnam: Black GIs' derogatory term for white GIs.
RAG Vietnam:	U.S. Army: River Assault Group.
Radio Nets:	Vietnam: (1) Free Net (2) Directive Net (3) Radio Listening Silence Net.
Radio Relay:	Vietnam: Network of radios working together to pass on information.
Rain Coats:	Vietnam: Euphemism for condoms.
Rain Gear:	Raincoat, trousers, poncho, boots, etc.
Rakes:	Combs with extra wide teeth favored by black GIs who wore Afro haircuts.
Railroad Tracks:	Army, Air Force, USMC: slang for two bars worn by a captain.
RAMP:	Korea II: Remote Areas Medical Program. U.S. effort in remote areas to combat Communist insurgents.
Rangers:	U.S. Army elite unit; motto: "Rangers lead the way." Designated LRRPs prior to 1969 in Vietnam.
Rank Insubordination:	Overt refusal to follow a direct order.
Ranks:	Enlisted Personnel E-1 through E-9.
Rapid Reload:	Adding ammunition fast into a weapon.
Rat Fuck:	Vietnam: Vulgarity to describe a mission of dubious necessity.
Rat Pack:	Vietnam: USAF commandos

Rat Patrol:	Vietnam, Korea II: Troops who patrolled in jeeps, normally armed with M-60 machine-gun. The latter patrolled 2nd Inf. Div. area of DMZ.
Ravens:	Nickname for USAF pilots flying in the "secret war" in Laos.
RD:	Vietnam: Rural Development (Teams).
Reaction Base:	ROK Term for reinforced bunker complexes on DMZ; manned day and night, normally by 36-man platoon.
Ready Rifles:	Vietnam; Nickname for 1st Bn. 198th Inf. Bde. Americal Division.
Ream Job:	GI term for getting shafted.
Rear Echelon Pogues:	Vietnam: Derogatory name for personnel supposedly far removed from the hazards of combat.
Rear March:	A unit turning 180 degrees and retracing its steps.
Rear Seat:	Gunner in a Cobra gunship, or an F-4 Phantom fighter-bomber.
Reception Center:	Military unit designated to receive incoming GIs for processing before assignment to a unit.
Rectal Defilade:	Vulgarity used to describe a bad decision or action.
Recon:	(1) Map (2)Aerial (3) Ground.
Recondo:	Vietnam: U.S. Army units that combined reconnaissance and commando activities.
Reconnaissance Patrol:	Korea I, Vietnam, Korea II: Small unit sent to scout for enemy troops, positions.

Recon by Fire:	Firing weapons into an area to see if the enemy responds.
Recruit:	USMC inductee.
Recruit Depot:	USMC processing center for new men.
Recycle:	Army BCT/AIT: Failure of a trainee to satisfactorily complete training and thus compelled to start entire process over.
Red Ass:	Korean War: USMC lingo for big trouble.
Red Ball:	Vietnam: High speed road or trail used by VC or NVA to move troops and supplies.
Red Baseball Caps:	Distinctive headgear worn by parachute riggers.
Redcatchers:	Vietnam: Nickname for 196th Light Inf. Bde. (1966- 1971).
Red Devils:	Nickname for Army's 5th Mech. Div.
Redeye:	U.S. Army: Shoulder-held anti-aircraft missile designed to hone in on an engine's heat.
Redistribute Ammo:	Squad leader's responsibility in firefight
Red Fenders:	Korea II: Distinctive color of fenders on vehicles used by Explosive Ordnance Demolition teams.
Reds:	Communists: Plentiful in Asia 1949-1975. (And still are).
Red Star cluster (at night):	Pyrotechnics signaling an impending enemy attack.
Redstone Arsenal:	Alabama site of U.S. Army Missile Command.
Refugee Camps:	Korea, Vietnam, Korea II: Wars forced millions of civilians into such camps.

Regimentation:	Philosophy of U.S. military to follow set rules and actions.
Reliable Academy:	Vietnam: 9th Inf. Div. booby trap indoctrination course.
Relief:	Replacing someone at an assigned duty station.
Remington Raiders:	Tongue-in-cheek description of men who manned typewriters. Also known factiously as "combat typists."
REMPs:	Rear Echelon Mother Fuckers.
Report:	Command given to a platoon leader standing in formation to report the status of his unit: Reply: "First platoon, all present and accounted for, sir!"
RP:	Vietnam: Release Point. Designated area where a unit crossed into hostile territory.
Research Space:	Section on USS Pueblo where 30-man intelligence crew operated to collect electronic data; designed to check NK radar installations and movements of enemy submarines in Sea of Japan.
Rest:	Troops in formation. Keeping right leg in place, but allowed to talk.
Retreat:	End of work day-normally about 1745 hours. Garrison troops caught outside at the sounding of retreat obliged to stop and hold salute until over.
Restricted Diet:	Vietnam: Fare of prisoners at LBJ (stockade) sent to administrative segregation or maximum security
Re-Up:	Re-enlisting for an additional term of service.

Reveille:	Wake-up call-normally 0515 hours in training; later hours at duty stations.
Reveille Gun:	Artillery piece fired at beginning of work day.
Revetments:	Steel concrete protection for U.S. military aircraft.
Ribbon Bar:	Small metal piece holding ribbons worn over left breast on a Class A uniform.
Rice Carriers:	Vietnam: Forced labor imposed on Montag nards by Viet Cong.
Rice Paddy Daddy:	GI jocular term mocking service in Asia.
Rice Raid:	Korean War: North Korean raids into South Korea prior to 25 June 1950.
Riki Tick:	Vietnam: See Most Riki Tick.
Rifle Salute:	Normally employed by a soldier on guard duty. Using the weapon to acknowledge approach of an officer involves moving rifle to a vertical position in front of the soldier.
Rifle Squad:	Basic infantry unit-normally 9 to 10 men.
RIFTED:	Reduction in Force.
Ring Knocker:	West Point graduate.
Rinky Dink:	Miscellaneous term for something of poor quality.
Ripcord:	Vietnam: Battle involving 101st AMD and NVA in 1970.
RITA:	Vietnam: Resistance Inside the Army. GIs who worked against U.S. policy.
Riverine Operations:	Vietnam: Mekong Delta area warfare that featured U.S. Navy patrol boats working with units of Army's 9th Inf. Div.

Rivers of Saigon:	See Cadence.
Roach Coach:	See Goody Wagon/Maggot Wagon.
Road Bound Army:	Military force dependent upon mechanized transportation.
Rockers:	Lower part of patch indicating rank. The more rockers the higher the rank.
Rocket Alley:	Vietnam: Area from Parrot's Peak to Bien Hoa-site of many enemy attacks.
Rocket Ridge:	Vietnam: Area south of Dak To.
Rocks Off:	GI slang for sexual intercourse.
Rock of the Marne:	Nickname for Army's 3rd Inf. Div. Stationed in Germany during Vietnam era.
Rock n' Roll:	Firing an M-16 on full automatic.
Rodong Shinmoon:	Korea II: North Korean Communist Party newspaper.
Roger That:	Radio/Telephone response indicating that the recipient of information understands and will carry out assignment.
ROK:	Republic of Korea.
ROKA:	Republic of Korea Army
ROKA Commandos:	South Korean Army personnel who undertook missions and raids against North Korea 1953-1971. More than 7,000 of these men were never heard from again.
ROKAF:	Republic of Korea Air Force
ROKMC:	Republic of Korea Marine Corps.
ROKNA:	Republic of Korea Navy.
ROKs in Vietnam:	ROKA White Horse and Tiger Divisions and Blue Dragon Marine Brigade, 1966-1972.

ROKA Rangers:	Korea II: Formed in all major commands after January 1968 unsuccessful attack against President Park Chung Hee.
Rolling Thunder:	U.S. bombing campaign against North Vietnam, 1965-1968.
Rome Plow:	Vietnam, Korea II: Large bulldozer with attached blades used to clear terrain.
RON:	Remain Overnight.
ROTC:	Reserve Officer Training Corps. Graduates earn an Army reserve commission as a 2nd lieutenant.
Round Eyes:	GI term for Caucasians, as opposed to the eye folds prominent in Asian populations.
RPD:	North Vietnamese machine-gun.
R&R:	Rest and Relaxation, Rest and Recreation, Rest and Recuperation. The reward service members often received halfway through their tour of duty. Some eligible for as many as 30 days, enabling them to return to CONUS.
RTO:	Radio-Telephone Operator
Rucksack:	German term for backpack. The pack worn by Army and Marine riflemen in the field.
Rules of Engagement:	Strictures on what was allowed by combat troops encountering enemy and civilian personnel regarding the use of deadly force.
RRU:	Radio Reconnaissance Unit. Cover for ASA to monitor radio frequencies.

RSM:	Marines Regimental Sergeant Major.
Run it up the flag and see if anyone salutes it:	Jocular GI phrase about bouncing an idea around and see if anyone supports around and see if anyone supports it.
RZ:	Vietnam: Reconnaissance Zone.

SIERRA

Sierra:	Nineteenth letter of phonetic alphabet.
Safe Conduct Pass:	Korean War: Paperwork issued to certain civilians to allow them to pass through tactical territory unmolested.
Saigon Commandos:	Vietnam: Derogatory term for rear echelon troops serving far from the action.
Saigon Cowboys:	South Vietnamese youth of military age who obnoxiously flaunted their civilian status.
Salt Tablets:	Vietnam, Korea II: Small pills taken by GIs in the field to prevent dehydration and sun stroke.
Salute:	Acknowledging and showing respect to a superior officer by touching side of hand to bill of cap and waiting for his return gesture.
S-A-L-U-T-E:	Acronym for determining composition of an enemy force. (1) Size (2) Activities (3) Location (4) Unit (5) Time (6) Equipment (7) Direction, if applicable.
Salute the Mountain:	Reveille in Korea, circa 1970
Sally Port:	Vietnam: Entrance to LBJ stockade.
Samo Samo:	Pidgin English spoken by GIs in Asia to indicate, "Same old, Same old."
Sampan:	Vietnam: Flat-bottomed boats used for transportation; commonly seen on rivers and coastal areas.
SAR:	Search and Rescue.

Satchel Charges:	Korea I, Vietnam, Korea II Bagged explosives detonated against barriers to allow entrance to an enemy position.
Say Again	Radio/Telephone Procedure, Meaning: Repeat last transmission.
Scout and Sentry Dogs:	Korea I, Vietnam, Korea II: Normally German Shepherds trained to detect booby traps, mines, enemy forces and to guard perimeters.
Screw Up A Wet Dream:	Put down for incompetent behavior.
Searchlight Operator:	Vietnam, Korea II: Large spotlights mounted on jeeps to illuminate enemy positions.
Searchlight Teams:	Vietnam: Small units assigned to seek out enemy positions.?
Second Looie:	Army, Air Force, USMC. Slang for a second lieutenant-the lowest officer rank.
Screening Operation:	Vietnam: Blocking and monitoring enemy movements near the DMZ.
SEALS:	U.S. Navy Elite Special Forces, stands for Sea, Air, Land. About 260 served in Vietnam.
Secret Clearance:	Security authorization of military personnel to handle classified documents. Ranked above confidential and below top secret classifications.
Section Eight:	Discharge from the military for psychological reasons.
Section Ten:	Discharge from the military for serious dereliction of duty.
Sector Sketch:	Drawing of a potential battlefield and the most likely avenues of attack.

Seduce and destroy missions:	Vietnam: Viet Cong targeting U.S. Marines by using attractive young women to lure them in to letting their guard down and following the women into the bush and often to their demise.
Sekigun:	Japanese Red Army Faction. Hijacked a Japanese airliner on 4 April 1970. Forced it to fly from Tokyo to Kimpo to Pyongyang. Group also responsible for detonating bombs around U.S. bases in Japan.
Selective Service:	Vietnam era: Federal government agency charged with conscripting young men for military service. More than 2 million drafted.
Selector Switch:	Device on automatic rifle that allowed firer to shoot single shot or multiple rounds.
Self-propelled 175-mm Gun:	Largest U.S. Army artillery piece that fired a 147-lb projectile 28 miles; estimated 250-foot kill radius.
Seoul City Sue:	Korean War: Female North Korean propagandist who broadcast in English, attempting to undermine morale of the GIs.
Send up the count:	Vietnam, Korea II: Technique of keeping track of men in a unit. Ex: In a squad of 10 men, last one in line is #10, next #9, 8, etc. At a halt, the squad leader passed down the word to "send up the count." Starting with last man the soldiers called out their number.

Sergeant Missile:	Korea II: Missiles deployed by U.S. Army.
SERTs:	Vietnam: Screaming Eagles Replacement Training School (101st AMD).
Service Cap:	Saucer-shaped cap worn with Class A uniform.
Service Stripes:	warded to military personnel with one stripe for every three years of service.
Service A's:	USMC dress uniforms.
Seven P's:	"Proper Prior Planning Prevents Piss Poor Performance."
Shack Gal:	Korean War: Term for prostitute.
Shake 'N' Bake:	Semi-jocular name for NCOs who gained rank through NCO school and Not through time in rank. Guided trainees through AIT.
Shakedown Inspection:	Surprise inspection of barracks/tent often conducted after midnight by upper echelon officers and NCOs to check for unsecured lockers, drugs, weapons, etc.
Shake hands with your best friend:	GI humor for handling penis.
Shamming:	Ducking out of duty.
Sharpshooter:	Badge awarded to soldier/marine sailor/airman firing for record; second most proficient score behind Expert and ahead of Marksman.
Shit Bird:	GI profanity
Shit Bricks:	Generic term for heavy duty stress.

Shit Burning Detail:	Vietnam, Korea II: Onerous job of disposing of human waste-often collected in large barrels with contents covered in gasoline and set afire.
Shit eating grin:	Vulgarity as in "Wipe that shit eating grin off your face!"
Shit for brains:	Derogatory put down of a GI who screwed up for some reason.
Shit from shinola:	Korean War: USMC vulgarity and put down.
Shit or go blind:	Vulgarity of nebulous definition.
Shit on a shingle:	GI term for chipped beef on toast-a common meal in training centers.
Shit's weak:	Vulgarity noting that individual in question was found lacking in some regard.
Shock:	Medical condition: a collapse of circulatory function; called greatest killer in combat.
Shoe Leather Express:	Slang for infantrymen.
Shook:	Korean War: USMC term for combat stress.
Short:	GI term for approaching end to active duty status.
Short Arm Inspection:	Korean War: Physical examination of male organ-normally checking for signs of venereal disease.
Short Sheet Bunk:	Juvenile prank pulled to harass a fellow GI by pulling back top sheet and tucking under bunk legs.
Short Time:	GI term for brief encounter with a prostitute.

Short-Timer's Calendar: Often risqué calendar prized by some GIs. Ex: a naked woman's body divided into 365 squares; the GI crosses off or colors in a square each day until DEROS Square #1 was the woman's vulva.

Short Tour: Vietnam, Korea II: Aka unaccompanied tour, normally 12-13 months. No family members allowed due to hazard and hardship in tactical areas.

Shot Over: Korea II: Artillery terminology for the impact area of a round.

Shot Record: Small booklet kept by service personnel to record inoculations administered at various duty stations.

Shoulder Patches: See patches.

Shower Shoes: Thongs or Flip-flops worn by GIs to prevent athlete's foot and other diseases prevalent in communal showers.

Sick Bay: U.S. Navy, Coast Guard term for dispensary.

Sick Call: Hours set aside for a GI to report to the infirmary or dispensary because of illness.

Sick Call Rider: Disparaging term for personnel who feigned illness to get out of training.

Signs of CBRL: (1) Yellow for gas (2) Blue for biological (3) White for radiological.

Sign out book: Korea II: Usually located at Company HQs. Mandatory for soldiers given passes or going on leave to sign name, rank, time out, time in, etc.

Simon Says:	U.S. Army: Training technique used to determine how closely trainees were listing to instructions. Ex: If drill sergeant says, "Simon says, about face," and the trainees do so, they are correct. But if drill sergeant blurts out, "about face" without the "Simon says" prelude, and they do so, they are chastised for not paying close attention.
Single Digit Midget:	Personnel with fewer than ten days before DEROS.
Sir:	Formal address to officers; in U5MC included senior NCOs.
SITREP:	Acronym for Situation Report
Sixth Infantry Division:	U.S. Army Jungle Warriors. Never activated during Vietnam era.
Skipper:	Navy, Coast Guard, USMC term for commander.
Sky Crane:	See C-54 helicopters.
Sky Jockeys:	USAF jet pilots.
Skyline Drive:	Korea II: Road near DMZ built by 11th Engineer Bn. in 1967.
Sky Soldiers:	Vietnam: U.S. Army airborne troops specifically members of 173rd Airborne Brigade.
Sky Troopers:	Vietnam: 1st Cav. Div. personnel.
Slack Jawed:	Stunned, nonplussed.
SLAM:	Vietnam: Acronym for "Search, Locate, Annihilate, Monitor."
Slant Eyes:	Derogatory term for Asians.

S LAR:	Korea II: Side-looking airborne radar used by U.S. Army OCI Mohawk aircraft used on combat-related surveillance along DMZ.
Sleeping Gas:	Sarin gas allegedly used by U.S. Army forces in Laos in 1970.
Slick:	GI term for Huey helicopter; specifically a chopper without exterior armaments. Used for troop transport, dust-offs, and miscellaneous duties.
Slicky Boys:	Korea II: Young men who often worked with prostitutes to rob and sometimes assault GIs.
Sling Arms:	U.S. Army/USMC: Carrying rifles over the shoulder using attached strap.
SLO:	Shitty little officer jobs
Slopes:	Vietnam, Korea II: Semi-derogatory term for indigenous Asians.
SMR:	Korean War: Special Money Request.
Smoke:	Vietnam, Korea II: Various colored grenades used to communicate a tactical situation. Ex: Red smoke indicated a "hot" LZ. Green smoke indicated a "clear" LZ. Yellow smoke indicated the location of friendly forces.
Smoke 'em if you've got 'em:	Self-explanatory.
Smoking lamp is out:	Old U.S. Navy term meaning "Douse the ciggie, mate!"
Smoky Bear Hats:	Distinctive headgear worn by USMC drill instructors and Army and Air Force drill sergeants. Army NCOs wore Blue/Black helmets.
Snake:	Vietnam era: Slang for Cobra gunships

Snake Eaters:	Special Forces personnel trained to live off the land, including catching, killing and eating poisonous snakes.
Snakes (Vietnam):	Seven poisonous reptiles included (1) Bamboo Viper (2) Blue Krait (3) Indian Cobra (4) King Cobra (5) Fer de lance (6) Habu (7) Sea snake.
Snatch:	Korea I, Vietnam, Korea II: Attempt to capture an enemy VIP.
Sneeze Sheet:	Plastic covering at head of a bunk to neutralize nasal discharge, slobber, etc.
Sniffed Out:	Korea II: GI term for detecting enemy personnel.
SOFA:	Korea II: Status of Forces Agreement. It gave South Korea authority to try U.S. GIs for crimes committed against Korean nationals. Signed in 1966.
SOI:	Signal Operating Instructions.
SOL:	Shit out of luck.
Soldier:	Member of U.S. Army, Reserves and National Guard.
Soldier's Notebook:	Small notebook purchased at PX and used by some GIs to take notes during lectures and instruction.
Son Tay Raid:	Vietnam: November 1970 effort by 30 elite military personnel to rescue POWS held in North Vietnam. Not successful.
SOP:	Standard Operating Procedure.
Sorry Excuse:	Put down of a particularly ineffectual decision or behavior.

Sorties:	Korea, Vietnam: Allied aircraft missions against enemy targets and planes.
South Tape:	Korea II: Two strand wire fence; top strand wrapped in white tape to mark southern edge of DMZ.
Soul Patrol:	Squad or unit composed primarily of black GIs.
Sounds like a personal problem:	Spoof of opportunity afforded overseas bound troops to discuss any problems before departure. SOP at Fort Lewis, WA. during Vietnam era.
Sound Off:	Command to commence counting cadence or to identify oneself in a tactical situation.
Spades:	Anchor used to stabilize howitzers (5,000-lb guns).
Special Action Force:	Vietnam: Similar to civic action units who provided medical, technological and agricultural assistance to indigenous personnel.
Special Court-Martial:	Military judicial proceedings dealing with misdemeanor charges. Conviction could result in a reduction in rank, one year in a military prison and a dishonorable discharge.
Special Forces:	U.S. Army elite unit. Motto: *De Oppressor Liber* (Free the oppressed) created in 1952.
Special Forces Tracking School:	Korea II: Facility located south of Kimpo AB.

Special Guerrilla U nits:	Laos: Hmong forces organized to fight Communist Pathet Lao and NVA forces.
Specialist:	U.S. Army enlisted rank. During Vietnam era included Specialist 4th Class to Special list 7th Class.
Special Operations Squadron:	Vietnam: USAF missions in UH-1F helicopters.
Speedy Express:	Vietnam: 9th Inf. Div. in Mekong Delta.
Speedy 4:	GI slang for Specialist 4th Class. A dangerous rank during Vietnam era; more E-4s were killed in action than any other rank. 84.1 percent of men KIA in Vietnam were E-6s and below.
Spider Holes:	Vietnam, Korea II: Dug out and camouflaged areas used to conceal enemy personnel.
Spit Shine;	Polishing footgear to the point of a mirror-like reflection; key ingredients being water and shoe wax.
Spooky:	See USAF C-47 aircraft.
Spoons:	Army cooks.
Spot Weld:	Area on the stock of an M-14 rifle where the soldier positioned his cheek each time he fired to maximize accuracy.
Squad:	Army/USMC tactical unit-normally 9-10 men.
Squad Leader:	Enlisted man-usually at least an E-4 who was in charge of both fire teams.

Squared Away:	Term indicating efficiency, order or preparation to accomplish mission at hand.
SRP:	Vietnam, Korea II: Short Range Patrol.
SR-71 Blackbird:	USAF ultra-high altitude intelligence gathering aircraft. During Vietnam era, craft deployed over North Vietnam and North Korea; based in Thailand and Okinawa respectively.
Stabo-Rig:	Vietnam: Equipment used to extract personnel from jungle areas, normally by helicopter.
Stack Arms:	Placing rifles together, often while soldiers in the field were engaged in other training.
Stand Down:	Order for a unit to pull out of the field, or shift to another mission or sector, often less hazardous.
Stand Retreat:	See Retreat.
Stand To:	Related to alert level. Ex 50% to 100% of available personnel awake, at posts and ready for action, depending on perceived threat.
Starched Fatigues:	Mandatory uniforms for soldiers marines and airmen, often when assigned to garrison duty.
Stars & Stripes:	Quasi-military newspaper. Pacific version based in Tokyo, Japan. Served armed forces in Far East, Southeast Asia and Western Pacific during Vietnam era.
State of War:	North and South Korea in 1969.
Stay alert, Stay alive:	Self-explanatory.

Stay-behind:	Korean War: Covert missions against North Korea by anti-Communist guerrillas; trained by U.S. Special Forces.
Stay off the skyline:	Spoof of survival training as in "Hey, dummy, don't make yourself an obvious target."
Steel Pot:	See Helmet
Stockade:	U.S. Army/USAF term for jail.
Stepped on the old Wing Wang:	Vulgarity often encountered in training- meaning that a trainee/recruit screwed up in some fashion.
STRAC:	Acronym for Strategic Air Force Command or Strategic Army Command. Army connotation meant first rate, ready to go, well-prepared, sharp looking.
STRATCOM:	U.S. Army's Strategic Command.
Strip Alert:	USAF: Aircraft on standby for immediate dispatch to deal with military emergencies.
Strobe lights:	Vietnam: Colored lights employed to signal approaching helicopters.
Styles of Saluting:	Taught in BCT and boot camp. Some variations: Rather than bringing side of hand to bill of cap or helmet, some cocked head to the right and bent into the salute.

Subdued Insignias:	At height of Vietnam War, U.S. Army opted to replace conspicuous rank markings on sleeves and colored shoulder patches with black/green patches, and small black pins. Brass belt buckles replaced by subdued black buckle on a black belt.
Sucking Chest Wound:	Common combat-related injury to torso that often caused the collapse of one or both lungs. First Aid focused on pressing a bandage to the chest or back to re-inflate the lung and keep the service member breathing.
Summary Court Martial:	Lowest in severity as far as punishment for an infraction.
Summer Alert Uniforms:	Korea II: Clothing worn by GIs during summer months- normally lighter than winter clothing.
Superior Officer:	In the chain of command, any rank higher than an EM.
Supernumary:	Extra good soldier.
Suppressive Fire:	Korea I, Vietnam, Korea II: Intense firepower to allow troops to maneuver, retreat, etc.
Super Surprise:	Vietnam: Face-to-face encounter with a heavily-armed enemy force.
Surveillance Team:	Vietnam: "Sneak and Peek" missions to observe enemy activities.
Survival Cards for Southeast Asia:	Resembled playing cards, but contained information about plants, animals, reptiles, etc. issued to troops for use in emergency survival conditions.

Swamp Stove:	Primitive cooking device-often made from large cans; sometimes used in the field to heat coffee, meals, etc.
Sweat Band:	Leather strip attached inside of helmet liner worn inside a steel pot.
Swift Sword of Death:	Patch worn by members of 173rd Airborne Brigade.
Swinging Richard/Dick:	Vulgarity for male organ incorporated into GI lingo. Ex: "I want every swinging Richard to listen up!"
Sympathetic Detonation:	Friendly booby trap, or wound from friendly forces, weapons, etc.

TANGO

Tango:	Twentieth letter of phonetic alphabet.
Tac Air:	Korea I, Vietnam, Korea II: USAF, U.S. Navy, USMC tactical air support for ground troops.
Tactical Liaison Officers:	Korean War: Individual officers assigned to assist Line Crossers infiltrating and exfiltrating North Korea.
Taeguk:	Highest military decoration in Republic of Korea.
Tag and Bag:	Korea I, Vietnam, Korea II: Term for identifying dead personnel and placing remains in a plastic body bag.
Taksan:	Japanese term for much, many, more; used by GIs in Korea.
Tanglefoot:	Vietnam: Barbed wire barrier placed about 12 inches off the ground around firebases to discourage enemy infiltration.
Tanks:	Large armored vehicles. During Vietnam era M48 and M60 models deployed in Asia and Europe.
TAOR:	Vietnam: Tactical Area of Operations.
Taps:	End of work day when lights were turned off in the barracks-normally 2300 hours or 11 p.m. Perhaps 2100 hours during training.
Tarmac:	Hard-surface combination of tar and macadam used to create solid foundation for airstrips, roads, etc.

Tasting Blood:	Vietnam era: Technique to determine condition of wounded enemy soldiers by examining blood samples left behind after a contact. A salt taste indicated a head wound; a sour taste a stomach wound; a sweet taste a leg wound.
Task Force 71:	Korea II: U.S. Navy's response to North Korean shoot down of an EC-121 in 1969 killing 30 sailors and one marine. The buildup included several aircraft carriers and escort ships that totaled 29 vessels.
Task Force 77:	Vietnam: U.S. Naval force in South China Sea 1964-1975. Always three aircraft carriers on station.
TDY:	Temporary Duty.
Technicians of War:	Vietnam: Self-identification of LRPs.
Ten Forty-Nine (1049):	Form for requesting transfer to another unit or MOs..
TFW:	Tactical Fighter Wing.
Thai Troops:	Soldiers from Thailand who served with U.S. troops in Korea I, Vietnam, and Korea II.
Thai Stick:	Vietnam: Potent type of marijuana smoked by some GIs.
Ten Percent:	Vietnam era: Percentage of men who volunteered for the draft.
There's something out there:	Korea II: Common phrase used by handlers of tracker dogs along the DMZ.
Third Herd:	Vietnam: Slang for 3rd platoon.

Third Tactical
Fighter Wing:

USAF wing of F-100 Sabre jets deployed in Vietnam from November 1965 to early 1970. Redeployed to Osan AB, Korea in 1971.

Thirty-Eighth
Parallel Fever:

Korea II: Term to describe determination of ROK troops to defeat the North Korean Army.

This is your weapon;
this is your gun; this
if for fighting and
this is for fun:

Ditty intended to teach trainees/recruits the proper terminology for their weapon. That is, don't call a rifle a gun; crude comparison to male organ.

Those:

Nonconformist soldiers.

Thousand Yard Stare:

Korea I, Vietnam: Term to describe a Marine who faced death too many times.

Three Day Pass:

Traditional 72 hour respite from military duty.

Three Forty-Seventh
(347th) TFW:

Korea II: USAF unit at Osan AB.

Three Hundred
Thousand (S300,000):

Vietnam: Cost to U.S. taxpayers to kill each Viet Cong, This according to Georgia Senator Richard Russell.

Three Postponements:

Vietnam: Viet Cong directive to unmarried cadre: (1) Falling in love (2) Getting married (3) Having babies.

Ticket Punchers:	Vietnam: Unflattering term for officers who wanted an in-country tour to ensure an upward trajectory of their careers. Officers often served six months in the field and six months in staff positions.
Tiger Cages:	Vietnam: Political prisoners kept by the GVN in small stone compartments 5x9 feet. By 1970, an estimated 9,900 civilian, military and political prisoners were being held.
Tiger Force:	Vietnam: Elite 173rd ABD and 101st AMD troops assigned to eliminate enemy infrastructure. Alleged use of black warfare circa 1967.
Tiger Land:	Vietnam era: GI nickname for Fort Polk, La. A main training base for combat troops.
Tiger Mountains:	Vietnam: Area southeast of Bong Son.
Tiger Stripes:	Vietnam: Jungle fatigues designed with black and yellow horizontal stripes. Worn by Rangers, and Special Forces and Tracker Teams only; not officially sanctioned by U.S. Army. Individual GIs paid indigenous tailors to make them.
Times Fuses:	Artillery shells timed to detonate 1-100 seconds after impact; used particularly for aerial bursts.
Tipsy 25:	Vietnam, Korea II: Radar used to detect enemy personnel and vehicles.
Ti-Ti:	Vietnam: GI pronunciation of Vietnamese word for "little."

Toc to Toc:	Tactical Operations Center. Communications at brigade or division level.
Toe Popper:	Vietnam, Korea II: GI term for M-14 anti-personnel mine. Designed to maim rather than kill. Version used by enemy forces.
Toilet Seat:	USMC term for marksman level of qualification, i.e. the lowest level of proficiency with a weapon.
Toms:	Vietnam: Black GIs name for black career officers who pressured black GIs to conform to military discipline.
Ton Son Nhut:	Vietnam: Main airport and airbase located outside Saigon.
TOP:	Short for Top Sergeant or Top Kick, meaning a high ranking NCO, usually a 1st Sergeant or Sergeant Major.
Topographical Symbols:	Maps: (1) Black represented man-made objects (2) Red, roads and built-up areas (3) Blue, drainage (4) Green, vegetation (5) Brown/Gray, elevation & relief contour lines.
Top Shirt:	See Top Sergeant.
T-O-T:	Korea I, Vietnam: Time Over Target.
Torque:	Vietnam, Korea II: GI term for Huey door gunner.
Tourniquet:	Strap device that allows a medic to apply pressure to a limb to stop the bleeding.
Tower Rat:	Vietnam, Korea II: GIs assigned as guards in towers around military bases.

133

Tracers:	Illuminated shells, normally one in every five live rounds. Designed to provide a rifleman with a perspective of where his rounds were striking. During Vietnam era, friendly troops fired red tracers; Communist forces fired green tracers.
Trail Watcher:	Korea I, Vietnam: Indigenous personnel assigned to observe the movement of enemy forces.
Trainee:	U.S. Army designation of a new soldier-first stage in molding a fighting man.
Trainfire:	Korea II: Marksmanship training for soldiers.
Transit Barracks:	Billet for personnel traveling between assignments or on leave.
Trees in Contact:	Vietnam: USAF terminology for unloading weapons on worthless targets.
Trench Foot:	Disease of the feet often caused by perpetual wetness and lack of hygiene. Infantry troops most susceptible.
Tri-Cap:	Abbreviation for Triple Capability. Ex, U.S. Army's 2nd Inf. Div. with armor, airmobile and ground units.
Trigger Control:	Technique for riflemen to smoothly pull trigger to avoid jerking motion and thus causing inaccurate strike of bullets.
Trip Flare:	Korea I, Vietnam, Korea II: Incendiary device designed to ignite when triggered by enemy personnel. Normally placed in close proximity to a perimeter.

Trip Tic:	Short for "Trip Ticket." Written authorization to take a military vehicle out of a compound on official business.
Triple Canopy:	Vietnam: Description of heavy jungle foliage, often having three layers of trees.
Tu dia:	Vietnam: Viet Cong warning to villagers about booby-traps.
Tuesday Lunch Bunch:	Vietnam: Gathering of President Johnson, Vice President Humphrey, Defense Secretary Robert S. McNamara and Secretary of State Dean Rusk to select military targets to be bombed in North Vietnam during Operation Rolling Thunder.
Tundra Mittens:	Korea I, Korea II: Gloves specially designed for cold weather duty; designed with a separate detached trigger finger for firing weapons.
Tunnels:	Vietnam, Korea II: Famous Tunnels of Cu Chi, an extensive tunnel network used by Viet Cong, located northwest of Saigon. In Korea, North Koreans dug a series of large tunnels under DMZ in 1960s and 1980s, some extending to outskirts of Seoul. Allegedly large enough for tanks to pass through.
Turtle:	Vietnam: GI term for a serviceman's replacement.
Two-Man Foxhole:	Korea I, Vietnam, Korea II: Protective hole dug to a depth of several feet to offer protection against enemy attack.

Twenty-Fifth (25th)
Inf. Div. 60th Scout
Dog Platoon:

Vietnam: Only unit with dogs specially trained for anti-booby trap work.

Twenty-First Rotation
Company:

Korea II: Thai Army unit headquartered at Camp Kaiser near DMZ.

Two-O-One File (201):

Official records kept on each service member. Contained a service member's MOS, training, education, fitness reports, awards, etc. Usually hand-carried between assignments.

TWX:

Tele Typewriter Exchange. Normally high priority messages sent from G-2 and G-3 sections to other units.

To Do Street:

Saigon, South Vietnam: Red Light District.

UNIFORM

Uniform: Twenty-first letter of phonetic alphabet.

UCMJ: Uniform Code of Military Justice. Rules that all military personnel were required to follow.

UIs: Korea II: Unidentified Individuals; deemed enemy combatants unless otherwise determined.

Ultra militarized Zones: Vietnam era: GIs' description of the reality of the military situation along the 17th and 38th parallels.

Under Arms: Carrying a weapon.

Uniforms: Assigned clothing worn by members of the military-idea of uniformity and creating a common bond.

Units Vietnam era: U.S. Army had 18 infantry and airmobile divisions and 4 armored divisions on active duty. USMC had 3 infantry divisions and air resources. USAF had 24 Air Wings, and U.S. Navy had more than 600 ships on active duty. U.S. Coast Guard had numerous vessels.

Units (Vietnam):	U.S. Army units were 1st Inf. Div., 4th Inf. Div., 9th Inf. Div., 23rd Inf. Div., 25th Inf. Div., 1st Air Cav. Div., 101st AMD., 11th Armored Cav. Regt. Brigade of 82nd ABD., 173rd AB Bde., 5th Mechanized Inf. Div. Bde. Also numerous support units. USMC had 1st and 3rd Divisions and air assets. 7th USAF; U.S. Navy had numerous blue water and brown water vessels, as did U.S. Coast Guard.
University of Maryland:	Vietnam era: Offered college classes to military personnel stationed In Vietnam, Korea, Okinawa, Japan, etc.
Urethritis, "Non-Specific":	Medical term for "The Clap" or gonorrhea.
URP:	Korea II: Unification Revolutionary Party. North Korean-sponsored insurgency in South Korea created in 1964. Largely neutralized by 1971.
USAF AC-47:	Vietnam: aka "spooky" aircraft armed with mini-guns.
U.S.:	Draftee during Vietnam. Also initials inscribed on U.S. Army equipment.
USARCSTA:	U.S. Army Reception Center.
USARPAC:	U.S. Army Pacific.
USAREUR:	U.S. Army Europe.

VICTOR

Victor:	Twenty-second letter of phonetic alphabet.
Valpack:	Korea I, Vietnam: USMC equipment.
Verbal Orientation:	Demonstrating training techniques.
Visual Orientation:	Demonstrating training techniques.
VFW:	Veterans of Foreign Wars.
Victor Charlie:	Vietnam: U.S. military phonetic term for VC or Viet Cong (Vietnamese Communists).
VC Chained to Trees:	Vietnam: Stories brandished to U.S. combat troops to indicate the level of Viet Cong fanaticism.
Victoria Cross:	Vietnam: Highest Australian award for military service.
Viet Nam Cong San:	Official name for Viet Cong.
Vietnam Orientation Order:	Preparation for a unit to engage in a tactical operation.
Vietnamese Roulette:	Vietnam: Tossing or threatening to toss VC suspects out of a helicopter to make them talk.
Village Rat:	GI who spent most of his off-duty time in nearest village that catered to GIs by selling alcohol, drugs, prostitutes, etc.
VOA:	Voice of America. Vietnam, Korea II: U.S. government-sponsored organization that transmitted pro-Free World information into Communist Bloc nations.
VOCO:	Verbal Orders of Commanding Officer.

VTR:	U.S. Army Vehicle Tank Retriever.
VI:	Korea I, Vietnam: Variable-timed flares.
VUNC:	Korea I, Korea II: Voice of the United Nations Command. U.S. Army psychological propaganda broadcasts into North Korea from 1953-1971.
VX:	See Nerve Gas.

WHISKEY

Whiskey:	Twenty-third letter of phonetic alphabet.
WACO:	Vietnam: U.S. Army MPs in Saigon Operation Center.
Wait a minute vines:	Vietnam: Ground-level foliage that caught GIs' boots and equipment that added to stress of moving through jungle terrain.
Wait One:	RTO communication indicating that one of the parties was being put on hold.
Wait Up:	Civilian term appropriated by GIs.
Walk on Water Card:	Vietnam: Alleged special identification card issued to U.S. Army Special Forces assigned to SOG.
Wall Locker:	High, vertical storage compartment used in barracks and hooches to store uniforms, equipment, personal effects, etc.
Warming Tents/Bunkers:	Korea I, Korea II: Designed to help line troops deal with inclement weather.
Warning Order:	See Patrol Order.
Warrant Officer:	Military personnel with specialized skills and authority through military training rather than an act of Congress. Example were helicopter pilots and co-pilots.
Wars of Liberation:	Southeast Asia: Vietnam, Laos, Cambodia.

War Room:	Vietnam: Nickname for G-3 Operations.
War Zones:	Vietnam: Country divided into four areas, A, B, C, D, with A closest to North Vietnam and working south. Also Korean War and Korea II 1966-1971. See Corps.
Wasted:	GI term for killing or being killed.
Water Bladder:	Large rubber container dropped in the field to supply troops with potable water.
Weapons Platoon:	Infantry unit equipped with heavy weapons such as mortars and heavy machine-guns.
Weapons Receipt card:	Card issued to GIs. When weapon checked out of arms room, card was kept by armorer; card returned to GI when weapon turned in.
Web Gear:	Pistol belt, frame, pack, straps, etc. Used to secure equipment.
Weekend Warriors:	Semi-derogatory term for National Guard or Army Reserves, or others not serving on active duty in a war zone.
WETSU:	USMC vulgarity: "We eat this shit up!"
Whirly Birds:	Korea I: USMC name for helicopters (Also eggbeaters and windmills).
White Mice:	Vietnam: GI term for South Vietnamese National Police, who wore white uniforms and helmets.
White Phosphorous or Willie Pete:	Vietnam: Non-lethal pyrotechnics used to communicate with other units, aircraft, etc.

White Pig:	Vietnam: Black GIs term for whites.
Why cultivate on your face what grows wild in the crack of your ass:	Vulgarity, sometimes used by senior NCOs to discourage facial hair worn by some young GIs.
White Star Cluster and Parachute Flares:	Vietnam: Pyrotechnic devices deployed to communicate with other units.
White Tigers:	Korean War: U.S. Army Special Forces soldiers who trained and sometimes accompanied anti-Communist North Koreans sent to infiltrate into and stage raids into North Korea.
Who has more fun, infants in the infantry or adults in adultery:	Semi-vulgarity, origin unknown; fairly humorous.
Wing Whippers:	Korea, Vietnam: USMC pilots.
Without Prejudice:	Officer reassigned; theoretically without damaging his career.
Wizzo:	USAF term for weapons service officer.
Wonju:	Shoot: Korean War: Huge artillery battle between U.S. 2nd Inf. Div. and CCP troops. Estimated 5,000 CCP troops killed.
World:	GI term for the U.S.
World of Hurt:	End result of some negative action.
World War II Barracks:	Common housing found in many training centers from WW II through Vietnam era.
Wonder Arches:	Korea II: USAF billets, made of concrete and steel0

Wounds:

Vietnam: (1) 0-60 days incapacitated stay in country. (2) 60-120 days, sent to Japan. (3) 120-days plus sent to CONUS.

Writing Up:

Vietnam era: Personnel guilty of attempting currency violation.

WTF:

"What the fuck!"

X-RAY

X-Ray: Twenty-fourth letter of phonetic
                                alphabet.

X- Ray: Seldom used in phonetic alphabet.

YANKEE

Yankee:	Twenty-fifth letter of phonetic alphabet.
Yaks:	Korean war: Russian-made warplanes.
Yankee go home:	Vietnam: Slogan directed at U.S. troops, more common in period 1969-1971. Often expressed following civilian casualties or crimes committed against Vietnamese by U.S. and allied forces
Yankee Station:	Vietnam: Area in South China Sea where many U.S. naval vessels (aircraft carriers) were stationed.
Ya owe it to yourself:	Vietnam: GI self-talk for dealing with stress of survival in a war zone.
Yellow Legs:	Korea I: USMC calf-high boots.
Yobo:	Korea II: Indigenous women who-in exchange for cash and other benefits acted as wives for GIs. Some free-lanced as prostitutes when "husband" was on duty.
You know what floats downstream:	GI acknowledgement that any major screw up will probably be blamed on lower ranking personnel.

ZULU

Zulu:	Twenty-sixth letter of phonetic alphabet.
Zapped:	GI term for killing or being killed.
Zero Out:	Term for GI to change duty stations or "zero out."
Zipper head:	Derogatory terms for Asians
Zone Tiger:	See Focus Retina.
Zoo:	Vietnam: Term coined by U.S. POWs for a North Vietnamese prison.